The
MYTH
of
RACE

JEFFERSON M. FISH, PhD

Cover photo: Hermandad-Friendship by Rufino Uribe, Grupo Babel
(Wikimedia Commons)

ISBN: 978-1-5399-8793-2
eISBN: 978-0-7867-5654-4

To Dolores, Krekamey, Chris, Jordan, and Jaden

CONTENTS

INTRODUCTION

Here's how it all began. I, a white psychologist from the Bronx, married an African American anthropologist from Brooklyn. Before long, we had a daughter and went off to Brazil as visiting professors for a couple of years. While there, we spent one month with the Krikati Indians, continuing my wife's fieldwork.

I became fascinated by the different way Brazilians think about race. Over time, this led me to an interest in understanding race cross-culturally, to immersing myself in the biological, sociocultural, and psychological literature, to doing research on the topic—comparing the concept of race in eight different cultures—and to publishing two academic books, *Race and Intelligence* and *The Concept of Race and Psychotherapy*.

Along the way, I learned much that was both fascinating and counterintuitive. I had grown up assuming that humans were divided into biological races (mainly Caucasoid, Mongoloid, and Negroid). Instead, I discovered that, not only had scientists long ago shown this version of reality to be false, but also that the apparently straightforward concept of race was actually a confused mixture of two different concepts. The first—biological race—simply doesn't exist in the human species. All that exists is gradual variation in what people look like, and in their genes, as you travel around the planet—with more distant populations appearing more different than closer ones. If you travel in different directions, the populations look different in different ways. The second concept—social race—is a set of cultural categories for labeling people based on how their ancestors were classified, selected aspects of what they look like, or various combinations of both. These sets of categories vary widely from one culture to another, as I documented in my research comparing the race concept in eight different cultures.

Within a single culture, such as in the United States, discussions of race also may lead to misunderstandings and exasperation because they entangle biological and cultural assumptions. Since race is such a charged topic, people often avoid talking about it. Many would rather live with their perplexity than raise questions that others—or they themselves—might view as prejudiced.

Disentangling biology and culture involves dispelling some myths. And doing so by exploring the race concept cross-culturally often leads to the unexpected—both to insights and paradoxes.

Books that talk about race generally speak about racial politics, discrimination, segregation, slavery, and a variety of topics that might be called the consequences of race. While these are important subjects, they avoid the topic of race itself. They rarely deal with questions such as the following:

"What is race?"

"Can you change your race?"

"I've heard that scientists say races don't exist. How is that possible when people from Norway, Nigeria, and Japan look so different from one another?"

"What identity issues do interracial people face?"
"How do other cultures think about race?"
"If races don't exist, how can the existence of racism be explained?"

This book focuses on understanding race itself, and on dispelling myths by providing clear and often surprising answers to such questions. Because the book deals with a series of topics, looking at race from different angles and through a variety of conceptual lenses, the chapters don't necessarily appear in a linear sequence. Some are relatively independent from one another, while others involve a degree of overlap and/or repetition. It is hoped, nevertheless, that the book forms an organic whole.

The first four chapters touch on many issues and pose many questions; and they provide succinct answers and explanations. The various sections of these chapters aim at clearing up confusions about race by disentangling biological issues from social and cultural issues.

The first chapter looks at the biological side of the race concept and explains why the human species doesn't have biological races. Chapter 2 looks at the cultural side of the concept, and examines why it is that some groups of people are considered races while others are not. Because biological and cultural ideas about race are jumbled together, confusions, misinterpretations, and awkward encounters are inevitable; and the third chapter is aimed at clarifying matters. Chapter 4 demonstrates the ways similar confusions permeate race categories in the American census. It shows how the categories have changed many times and explains how a simple solution could clarify matters in future censuses.

The last four chapters paint broader pictures, integrating perspectives from the first four, bringing in new information, and including some of my own experiences at home and abroad.

Chapter 5 begins with a puzzling question about racial identity from my family: Why did my daughter's Brazilian boyfriend say he isn't black, and my daughter say she is, even though he is darker than she? In order to answer the question, the chapter discusses additional, relevant biological and cultural information. Solving the puzzle leads to a more general discussion of the concept of race—in different cultures, as applied to children of intermarriage, and as confronted by immigrants. Chapter 6 explores the race/IQ controversy and explains why claims of biologically based racial differences in intelligence are scientifically meaningless. In doing so, it explains key IQ-relevant issues, such as heritability, twin studies, different kinds of minorities, and the role of formal education. The chapter also offers suggestions for ways parents can raise smarter kids.

Chapter 7 makes use of President Barack Obama's upbringing for comparative purposes. Obama has an unusual background and complex identity: black and white; American and Indonesian and Kenyan; life in Hawaii, Indonesia, California, New York, Cambridge, Chicago, and Washington. His life offers a well-known example for disentangling issues of biology and culture, and I have used him as an illustration in various ways in several chapters. In particular, the idea for Chapter 7 arose from similarities between the family he grew up in and the one my wife and I raised our daughter in. These include life as a child of black and white parents, and living in another country where the mother did anthropological research. Obama's book, *Dreams from My Father*, gave a child's-eye view of his childhood. This chapter, *Dreams from My Daughter*, offers a parent's-eye view of raising a daughter under similar circumstances. It is aimed at illuminating questions faced by children of intermarriage, including biculturalism and issues of racial and cultural identity.

The last chapter reviews and extends earlier discussions of reasons that the human species has no biological races. It compares the spread of humans out of Africa over tens of thousands of years with the spread of the race concept out of Europe over a few hundred years. It also explains why the race concept is so durable despite scientific evidence to the contrary.

CHAPTER 1

The Myth of Caucasoid, Negroid, and Mongoloid Races

Discussions of race often confuse biology and culture. The sections of this chapter begin to disentangle the two by shedding light on the biological side of the race concept.

Is There Only One Race, the Human Race?

People sometimes say, "There is only one race—the human race."

I like the sentiment, emphasizing our common humanity; and I share the feeling. But there is a logical problem with it. For the word *race* to have any meaning there would have to be more than one. (*Race*, as the term is commonly used, is a social category—but that is a subject to be dealt with later.)

When it comes to human beings, the biological word we are looking for is *species*. A species is a group of organisms that can breed with one another and produce fertile offspring.

Homo sapiens is a species because people from anywhere on the planet can—and with modern transportation some actually do—breed with others from anywhere else, no matter how far away, and have fertile offspring.

Humans and sheep are two different species because, even if a human were to try to impregnate a sheep, as some are reported to have done, the attempt would fail.

Donkeys and horses are also two different species, and they provide an example that is enlightening in unexpected ways. They are close enough genetically to interbreed and produce offspring—mules. Mules are not an exception to the definition of species, however, because mules are sterile. Thus, no matter how many mules may be born, donkeys and horses remain reproductively separated—they cannot merge into a single species.

The Portuguese and Spanish origin of the word mule, which goes back hundreds of years before modern science, is also the source of the word *mulatto*. That is, people in pre-scientific agrarian Europe, who knew nothing about species or culture, believed there was a fundamental similarity between the sterile offspring of donkeys and horses and the fertile offspring of Europeans and Africans.

Among the apes, the chimpanzees and bonobos are biologically closest to humans. Like us, apes have no tails, while monkeys who are more distant genetically, do. Interestingly, humans are more similar genetically to chimpanzees than donkeys are to horses.

This raises the obvious questions: Could a human and a chimp make a baby? And if so, would it grow up to be fertile or sterile? I have asked some biologists, and they have told me the following: no one has published an answer because the experiment would be unethical. Scientific curiosity being what it is, someone somewhere may have tried it (in a test-tube, but not in bed). So some individual may know the answer, but Science does not.

So, as far as *Homo sapiens* is concerned, and barring evidence to the contrary, I would go with the statement, "There is only one species, the human species."

Why Do So-Called Racial Features Vary Gradually?

OK, so humans are one species. But doesn't the human species have different races—Caucasoid, Negroid, and Mongoloid—that mix together to get the varieties of humans we see today? Actually, no. Science has shown that this view is wrong. Understanding this begins with understanding that so-called racial features, such as skin color and hair form, vary gradually.

Let's start by noting the difference between what might be called *social race*—using the word *race* to classify people by what they look like, or by their ancestry, or by some other social criteria—and *biological race*. In contrast to biological races, social races do exist—though racial systems of classification differ from one culture to another and form the basis for unequal treatment of differently categorized groups.

Among humans' many physical features, Americans only consider some of them to be racial. For example, we think of skin color, but not body shape, as racial. Furthermore, the traits that Americans consider racial are variable (e.g., skin color varies from dark to light) rather than fixed (e.g., the mistaken belief that one biological race has dark skin color and another has light skin color). Why is that? Why are the traits that we think of as racial variable? Answering the question requires an understanding of breeding populations and clines.

Suppose you have a breeding population (members of a species that breed among themselves more than they do with other populations) of humans that has a high percentage of a certain gene. Let's call them Population 1—think, for example, of a geographically isolated village prior to modern transportation. At some distance there is another human population that we will call Population 2. Since there is contact between the two populations, including sexual contact, over time some people in Population 2 will also have the certain gene. However, because members of Population 1 don't breed with those in Population 2 as often as they do among themselves, the percentage of people with the gene in Population 2 will never be as high as in Population 1. At another distance even further away from Population1 is Population 3. Following the same logic, the gene will spread to Population 3, but its frequency will never be as high as in Population 2. And so on, for populations 4, 5, 6, and others—the further from Population 1, the lower the percentage of people with the gene.

This gradual geographical change in the frequency of a gene (or, for that matter, a visible trait like body shape or skin color) is known as a *cline*—think of words like *decline* or *incline*.

So the reason that so-called racial features are variable rather than fixed is that their distributions are clinal. (Clinal distribution applies to traits whether they are determined by one or many genes—the further away, the fewer people have the genes, and, therefore, the less there is of the trait.)

As with topographical maps, where dark brown signifies great altitude and dark green signifies sea level, it is possible to make maps of gene frequencies, or the frequencies of visible traits, where different colors represent different frequencies instead of different altitudes.

You can make a bunch of these maps of the planet, each for a different gene or trait; if the maps are transparent, you can place them on top of one another. If races existed, then they would all pretty much coincide. But they don't. Different traits go off in different directions, and are found together or separated in different parts of the world.

Why is this? The reason is to be found in human history and pre-history. Unlike species, which can be roughly represented as a branching tree because they have been reproductively isolated for a long time, humans are a relatively new species, without a lot of genetic variability, and travel all over the place and mate with one another wherever they are. Rather than a branching tree, the history of human populations would more accurately be depicted as a tangled web or network or lattice. The hodgepodge of clines going every which way reflects the chaotic human past of groups spreading out to populate the planet, breaking apart, coming together, and having gene frequencies affected by marriage rules and sexual taboos, not to mention war, disease, and natural disasters.

In brief, human physical variation is clinal, and because the various clines do not coincide, it is not racial.

Where Did the Idea of Geographical Races Come From?

Since the idea of distinct geographical races is still widely believed, despite the clinal nature of human variation, it is worth understanding its origins.

When Europeans conquered the New World five centuries ago, they wanted to know whether the peoples they encountered were fully human and descended from Noah; and the Church decided that they were and did. Later, the Enlightenment brought the discovery of striking anatomical similarities between humans and apes, and the accurate proposal that variations among distant groups of humans could be explained by differences in their social upbringing. By the late eighteenth century, however, this view was replaced by an ideology of natural inequality among groups that led to the idea of "race." Several scholars have argued that this biologized meaning of race arose in the American colonial experience and then spread to European thought and beyond.

Mixing social behavior with physical appearance has been a part of the concept of race since its inception, and was part of Carl Linnaeus's racial descriptions published in 1758. Linnaeus, famed for classifying biological species, is regarded as the father of taxonomy; but his categories of humans—europaeus, africanus, asiaticus, and americanus were embarrassingly ethnocentric. Europeans, not surprisingly, were described in positive terms as "gentle, acute, inventive, and governed by laws," while Africans were "crafty, indolent, negligent, and governed by caprice"; Asians were "severe, haughty, miserly, and ruled by opinions"; and Native Americans were "obstinate, merry, free, and regulated by customs." A few decades later, Johann Blumenbach increased the number of varieties of race to five—Caucasian, Ethiopian, Mongolian, American, and Malay. Other scientists came up with different and often larger numbers of races, as they discovered inconsistencies in the data and unsuccessfully tried a variety of schemes for drawing boundaries around segments of continuous variation.

As we now understand, because Western Europe is so distant from the Americas and West Africa, and because of Europeans' limited awareness of peoples from regions in between, the illusion that humans came in qualitatively different subgroups was easy to sustain. In the English colonies, in particular, these differences in appearance were capitalized on to provide a biological rationale for innate differences among the groups. This, in turn, provided a justification for European economic exploitation of the other groups in convenient ways (rationalized as appropriate to their differing forms of inferiority)—taking the labor of Africans by enslaving them and confiscating the land of Native Americans by limiting them to reservations.

Are There "Racial Syndromes" of Features That Go Together?

Returning to the theme of the nonexistence of biological races, the mistaken view I want to elaborate on next is the idea of "racial syndromes." To Americans the key elements are skin color, facial features, hair form and color, and eye color; and these are believed to characterize the Caucasoid, Mongoloid, and Negroid "races." Actually, these eighteenth-century terms have long been dismissed as unscientific by sociocultural and biological anthropologists and by evolutionary biologists—though the word hasn't necessarily gotten out to non-specialists in other disciplines.

Instead of the various visible features clumping together, they vary separately. This is easy to verify wherever you can find a broad range of people, such as the New York City subway. All you have to do is make up a chart and discreetly rate the people you see for skin color, hair form, hair color, eye color, the ratio of nose width to length, and lip thickness. You will quickly discover that all combinations exist.

If there were racial syndromes, then a "totally white" person would have very light skin color; blond, straight hair; blue eyes; narrow nose; and thin lips. A "totally black" person would have very dark brown skin color; black, tight curly hair;

dark brown eyes; broad nose; and thick lips. And people in between would have, to a correlated degree, tan skin color; light brown eyes; brown, wavy hair; and intermediate nose and lip forms. Of course, such people do exist, but so do people with all the other possible combinations.

For example, some people have half "black" features and half "white" features, and no in-between features. In the United States, they are all considered black, but in northeastern Brazil they are considered neither black nor white, and there are various names for them, depending on what they look like. Thus, someone with light skin color, blond tight curly hair, broad nose, and thick lips would be called a *sarará*, and someone with dark skin color, straight black hair, brown eyes, narrow nose, and thin lips would be called a *cabo verde*.

These cultural differences in classification show that race is a cultural category rather than a biological one.

Not only can one see evidence that the idea of racial syndromes is incorrect by looking at diverse populations—it is obvious in many African American families. Ranking the members on separate scales of skin color, hair form, and other visible features will often produce quite varied results. For example, one person has the lightest skin color, another has the straightest hair, another the narrowest nose, and so forth.

In summary, another reason races don't exist is that so-called racial traits do not vary together in "racial syndromes."

Powers of Two and Human Population Growth

In addition to clinal variation and the nonexistence of racial syndromes, here is one more reason that the human species has no races—this time using logic, the powers of two, and the facts about human population growth.

Every person has two biological parents, four biological grandparents, eight biological great-grandparents, and so on. In ten generations, that adds up to 1,024 ancestors, and thereafter, using computer jargon, we're dealing in thousands, or kilo-ancestors. Twenty generations mean 1,048,576, and thereafter millions or mega-ancestors. Thirty generations mean 1,073,741,824, and billions or giga-ancestors. Forty generations mean 1,099,511,627,776, and trillions or tera-ancestors.

Before modern medicine and public health, people didn't live very long and reproduced when they were young. To be conservative in our estimates, however, let's count twenty-five years per generation. For example, forty multiplied by twenty-five equals one thousand, which means—as we have calculated—that a thousand years ago, every human alive today has more than one trillion ancestors. Since modern humans have been around for about 200,000 years, it is easy to see that—adding another three zeros every ten generations, or 250 years—this accounting gives us more human ancestors than there are atoms in the universe.

As if that weren't bad enough, there is another problem—the facts go in the opposite direction from the math. While the calculation of ancestors gives us numbers that explode in magnitude the further back in time we go, the actual history of the human species has been just the opposite. That is, we are actually undergoing exponential growth in the size of the human population, so that the further back in time you go, the smaller the number of humans.

To be specific, it took nearly the entire two hundred thousand years of our existence—roughly until 1800—for the world population to reach one billion. In a little more than a century—by the 1920s—it reached two billion. By 1960, despite World War II and numerous natural and human catastrophes, there were three billion of us. Since then, we have been adding one billion people every twelve to fourteen years, with estimates that the global population reached seven billion in 2011 or 2012.

How can we reconcile this contradiction?

There is one clear answer. They are all the same people!

That is, your biological great-great-great-great-*et cetera* grandparents and my great-great-great-great-*et cetera* grandparents, and for that matter the great-great-great-great-*et cetera* grandparents of everyone on the planet today are the same people. Whatever the superficial differences in what we look like, in biological terms we are all closely related—too closely related for the human species to have races.

The Main Reason Races Don't Exist

So far, we have considered several reasons that there has been, for about a half-century, a consensus among specialists—biological anthropologists and evolutionary biologists—that biological races do not exist in the human species. However, the scientific consensus stems mainly from overwhelming and convergent evidence from genetics and archaeology that documents the actual history of the human species.

Anatomically modern humans originated in East Africa about 200,000 years ago, having diverged from earlier forms. Their initially small numbers grew over time but were reduced to near extinction about 70,000 years ago, perhaps as the result of a global climatic catastrophe following the eruption of the Toba supervolcano in Indonesia. At that relatively recent date in human evolution, the great bulk of whatever genetic variability had developed by then was wiped out.

While new research is constantly revising the dates for the first human migrations out of Africa, it is possible that it was not until after that catastrophe that the first humans left for Eurasia, taking with them much less genetic variability than the limited amount previously extant in Africa. In any event, African populations contain two hundred thousand years of human genetic variability. In contrast, Eurasians, because they are descended from the small and unrepresentative numbers who left Africa, had much less genetic variability at the outset, and have had only one-half to one-third as much time for it to increase.

About fifteen thousand years ago during an ice age, much of the Earth's water was in the form of ice, leaving ocean levels substantially lower. As a result, there was a land bridge where the Bering Strait now separates Alaska from Siberia. A small number of humans crossed it into the New World. They brought with them a small proportion of the limited genetic variability that then existed in Eurasia.

Thus, instead of the supposed existence of different races on different continents, we see that there are actually three regions of differing genetic variability. The great majority of human genetic variability is in Africa, where we have been evolving for 200,000 years. There is some genetic variability in Eurasia, where we have been evolving for 60,000 to 100,000 years. And there is relatively little genetic variability in indigenous populations of the New World, where we have been evolving for about 15,000 years.

If the human species did have biological races, they would all be in Africa.

It is easy to see biological variability in Africa—for example, the Mbuti pygmies are very short, and the Masai are very tall. Despite these obvious differences, Americans classify them both as belonging to the same "race" because they have dark skins. This is an illustration of the way "race" is cultural classification masquerading as a biological one.

However, as the above discussion indicates, there just isn't enough variability among humans to produce biological races. And that is the main reason races don't exist.

Why Norwegians, Nigerians and Japanese Look So Different

Despite all that has been discussed thus far, the questions still get asked, "How can you say there are no races, when people from Norway, Nigeria, and Japan look so different from one another? And how can you explain the existence of racism, if races don't exist?"

Some people (who haven't read this book) may have heard that scientists say the human species has no races; but because this seems to contradict their everyday experience, they may dismiss it as an example of political correctness. Not so—it is real science! But, as has already been pointed out, to understand what scientists are talking about, we need to distinguish between biological races—which don't exist—and social races. Social races are all too real and have a long and unfortunate history, but there is no genetic test for a person's social race any more than there is a genetic test for religion or political affiliation or other social category.

Even though skin color and hair form are biologically based, grouping them into races is a social classification. For example, we could invent a race of people with large ears and small feet, and another race of people with small ears and large feet. These are also visible biological features, but it is easy to see that races created from such features are social rather than biological categories.

As we have seen, the human species began in Africa and continued to evolve there for at least one hundred thousand years before the first people left for Eurasia. This means that, if we trace our American ancestry back far enough, we are all African Americans. It also means that the great majority of human genetic variability is in Africa.

We simply haven't been around long enough and in separate enough groups to develop biological races. Humans are quite homogeneous genetically when compared to large territorial mammals such as wolves. (Wolves have several times as much genetic variability as humans.)

What people look like varies gradually around the planet. The further apart two populations are, the more dissimilar they appear. If you go in different directions, the people appear different in different ways. The reason that Norwegians, Nigerians, and Japanese look so unalike is that Norway, Nigeria, and Japan are so distant from one another—not because they represent pure forms of three races.

India, for example, is roughly midway among the three countries. It has about 1.2 billion people—greater than the entire population of the planet two hundred years ago. A lot of people in India have black, straight hair like East Asians, dark skin like Africans, and European facial features. That's a lot of exceptions to the notion of biological races among humans, and a lot of evidence for the gradual change in what populations look like as they get more distant from one another.

The distinction between (nonexistent) biological races and social races, also explains how there can be racism in a world with no races. Racism is a socially learned response to socially defined races.

CHAPTER 2

The Myth that a Person's Race Cannot Change

This chapter looks mainly at the cultural side of the race concept. It examines a number of different categories of people and considers why it is that some are considered races while others are not. Interestingly, racial and ethnic categories turn out to be quite flexible.

Is Caucasian a Race?

Let's begin with white folks. What should they be called?

Well-intentioned people who want to avoid giving offense or who want to appear erudite or scientific often say *Caucasian*. It is a big word, which gets additional authority from being capitalized.

Caucasian is all over the Internet. I came across the word in products to "dread Caucasian hair," *Caucasian, The New Minority* T-shirts, and Caucasian flesh-tone paints. The largest category is children's toys. These include a Caucasian Barbie and a variety of other name brand and handmade dolls representing ages from infancy through adulthood with all kinds of shoes, brushes, purses, and other accessories for the Caucasian dolls, and even a dollhouse for a Caucasian family.

People seem to think that Caucasian is a modern scientific term. Actually, it was coined in the eighteenth century by the German physician Johann Friedrich Blumenbach and published in his MD thesis in 1776. Blumenbach studied skulls from different parts of the world in an attempt to make geographic generalizations about what we now call culture. In much the same way, phrenology developed a few decades later to make psychological generalizations about individuals based on the bumps on their heads.

The Caucasus Mountains span Georgia, southern Russia, and other southern parts of the former Soviet Union. Blumenbach chose the word Caucasian to refer to Europeans because he thought the skull of a woman from that region was the most beautiful. I am not making this up. As I imagine Blumenbach contemplating his Caucasian skull, I find my mind wandering to Hamlet contemplating another skull, "Alas, poor Yorick! I knew him, Horatio," or Pygmalion falling in love with his statue of Galatea.

I had a student who grew up in the former Soviet Union. She told me that Russians have a term they use to refer to Caucasians. It is *black*. You can imagine how perplexed she was, on coming to the United States to discover not only that *Caucasian* means *white* here, but that we think that by calling people *Caucasian* we are being scientifically correct.

Evolutionary biologists and biological anthropologists, the key scientific specialists, abandoned the term long ago. However, *Caucasian* still keeps popping up—not just in the mass media, but in less specialized scholarly and scientific journals as well. The scientists in the know have not managed to get the word out to colleagues in other fields, or to the general public.

This is the problem with race terms in general. We think that we are speaking about biological groups, when in reality we are referring to culturally defined groups. Instead of *Caucasian*, I would suggest that we use terms that don't sound scientific—such as *white*—or that are explicitly cultural, such as *European American*.

Are Latinos a Race?

When I was in the first grade in Manhattan—could it really have been in the late 1940s?—I had a playmate named Mariano. His parents came from Puerto Rico and spoke little English, which was just fine with my mother, who had been a Spanish major. Back then, most Spanish speakers in New York were Puerto Rican, and *Puerto Rican* was the generic racial term used to refer to all Latin Americans. Both whites and blacks might—with no sense of irony or incongruity—utter this sentence: "He's a Puerto Rican from Mexico." Later, perhaps because increasing numbers of immigrants from Cuba, the Dominican Republic, Mexico, and other Latin American countries made the term untenable, *Hispanic* became the new word to refer to the same vaguely defined range of people.

I have a problem with the term *Hispanic*. I lived in Brazil for a couple of years, as I mentioned earlier—a transformative experience—and I return there periodically. I consider Brazil my second culture. I have close friends there, including, sadly, a few who have died—bringing home the meaning of "lower life expectancy in developing countries." Brazil has half the population of South America and occupies more than half its landmass. Nearly everyone there speaks Portuguese. If I may be permitted a bit of Brazilian ethnocentrism, I would point out that the people of South America are predominantly Portuguese-speaking— especially since tens of millions of people in the rest of the continent speak Quechua, Aymara, Guarani, and other indigenous languages as their first, primary, or only language. *Hispanic* (from *Hispania*, which means Spain in Latin) suggests Spanish-speaking, and when Brazilian friends come to visit, they complain of interactions such as the following:

"Where are you from?"

"Brazil."

"How interesting. My son is taking Spanish in high school."

So *Latino* feels much better to me, because it includes Brazilians. In addition to language, however, there is also the question of race.

In American folk terms, whites, blacks, and Latinos are three races, as in "He's not black, he's a Latino," or "She's not white, she's a Latina." And most Americans would agree that discrimination against Latinos is racial discrimination. A century ago, Italians came to the United States, and now their descendants are white. At the same time, other Italians went to Brazil, and when their *branco* descendants visit me, they are Latinos—not quite as white as Italian Americans.

The 2000 and 2010 censuses declared that Latinos can be any race—creating the hierarchical paradox that Latinos are a race that can be any race. Most Mexicans have more New World ancestry than most Native Americans—but Mexican Americans can't say they are Native Americans because their ancestors weren't born in the United States. This is just one of the reasons that "Other" has been the most rapidly growing census category.

Given all the complications that language, ethnic classification, and racial classification create for Latinos in the United States, I sometimes wonder what cultural identity Mariano developed as he grew into adulthood.

Who Is Asian?

An Iranian immigrant to the United States described to me his first contact with American racial concepts. He had to fill out a form and label himself with one of the listed options. When he chose Asian, he was told, "You aren't Asian."

How odd. As far as he was concerned, Iran is a large country in Southwest Asia; you can hardly miss it. It is larger than France, Germany, Italy, and the United Kingdom combined (and its population is larger than that of France or Italy or the UK). How could he not be Asian?

In the United States, Asians are a minority group. Much more than half of the earth's the population is in Asia, which makes non-Asians—everyone on all the other continents and islands combined—minorities. Our majority traces its roots to Europe, which we have promoted to a "continent"; but a look at a map suggests that it would be more accurate to view Europe as a peninsula on the Asian continent.

Racial concepts are folk concepts and change with changing conditions. *Asian* in the United States has traditionally meant East Asian, especially Chinese and Japanese. With increased immigration from many countries, the expanded category also includes Southeast Asians. In contrast, as the Iranian example indicates, Southwest Asians seem to be excluded from our Asian folk concept and are often thought of as Arabs—though this is inaccurate geographically, linguistically, and culturally.

With regard to South Asians—immigrants and their descendants from India, Pakistan, Bangladesh, and Sri Lanka—as their numbers have grown, the ways Americans have categorized them and they have classified themselves have been in flux. Are they white, black, Asian, or something else? Much more than one-fifth of the world's population is in South Asia, but their relatively small numbers in the United States have only recently grown to create a category "problem" in our racial labeling. As a "solution," there are signs that a *Desi* identity is developing among South Asian Americans, providing strength in numbers in a parallel to a Latino identity. But it is unclear whether the term *Desi* will be adopted by other Americans, or whether South Asians will eventually be viewed as "different from Asians," "a kind of Asians," or simply "Asians."

There are obvious disadvantages to classifying people by race—including stereotyping, the potential for discrimination, and promoting cultural misunderstandings through mislabeling. However, the naïveté of American outsiders, especially regarding the horrors of events in Asian history, creates space for people within a racial category to ignore cultural prohibitions. Thus, a marriage between a Chinese American and a Japanese American would not raise white eyebrows, because they are "both Asian." The same goes for a marriage between the children of immigrants from India and Pakistan ("both South Asian")—or, to pick a recent European example, Serbia and Croatia ("both white").

Over time, it is likely that answers to the American questions "Who is Asian?" and "What does it mean to be Asian American?" will continue to change. And might the merging of ethnicities be a signal that certain historical antagonisms are fading, at least in America today?

Why Isn't There a French Race?

There are all kinds of Latinos from all kinds of places. Puerto Ricans are from a territory of the United States; and we also have Spanish speakers and their descendants with origins throughout Mexico, Central America, South America, and the Caribbean, as well as Portuguese speakers and their descendants from Brazil—and smaller numbers from elsewhere. Latinos, with or without Iberian family names, are quite varied in what they look like and have ancestries traced to and blended from all corners of the Earth, especially from Europe, Africa, and the New World. Latinos may come from countries that have in the past been at war with each other, but most Americans consider them all part of a common "race."

There are also all kinds of French speakers and their descendants in the United States, but there is no folk term such as *Latino* to group them into a "racial" category. There are *québécois* and *acadiens* from Canada, and Cajuns in Louisiana descended from *acadiens*. There are also many immigrants and their descendants from the French Caribbean. These include Haiti, a country that has been independent from France nearly as long as the United States has been independent from England; Martinique and Guadeloupe, which are parts of France just as Hawaii is part of the United States; and other islands whose status is more analogous to that of Puerto Rico. Smaller numbers come from other former French colonies around the world. Many people have French surnames, and they are every bit as varied in what they look like as are Latinos. Why don't we group them together into a French "race"?

Interestingly, the French have a category, *la francophonie*, which unites these diverse peoples. It means more than just communities of French speakers, as it attempts to imply some shared essence that creates a unity of values and identity. (There is even an International Organization of the Francophonie, with dozens of member countries, not all of which are French speaking.) It is easy to see that such a cultural category is in the interest of France, and the prestige of "Frenchness" is a global marketing triumph. For example, in the 1970s the Brazilian upper class would send its sons to America to learn English and business, and its daughters to France to learn French and become refined.

One difference between Latinos and French-affiliated people in the United States is numbers. There are so many Latin Americans that it serves the interest of the majority to group them together for reference purposes; and as minorities it is also in their interest to band together for mutual support under a shared rubric.

Our history of slavery led to the development of racial folk classifications, with white as an exclusionary category, based on ancestry. Traditionally, in the United States, a person who looks white but has "black blood" isn't really white. Because Americans think in racial terms, Latinos and other minority groups get racial labels. Racial categories are socially constructed and change over time. Irish, Italian, and Eastern European Jewish immigrants weren't always considered white, but now they are. We haven't constructed a French race in the United States because, quite possibly, there simply aren't enough French-affiliated people here.

Is Barack Obama Black or Mixed?

Barack Obama's election as president symbolized for many a triumph over prejudice. But for some, the question remains: Is he black?

As with all such questions, it depends on what you mean by black.

One way to reach an answer is to list the principal meanings of black and respond to each one. That way you can choose the meaning you are interested in and get your question answered. In addition to deciding how to classify Obama in terms of a specific criterion, this exercise also helps to understand our culture's various meanings of black.

It is also possible to go further, comparing the meanings of various racial terms, here and in other cultures, and see what additional insights they offer.

When I was growing up, and certainly in my parents' generation as well, Barack Obama would have been considered black—though the words Americans used to denote people now called African American changed over time from colored to Negro to black. Today, most high school and college students I've met would call Obama mixed. This is a real change in meaning, moving people of diverse parentage out of one purportedly biological category of race ("If he has black blood, he's black") and into another ("If he's black and white, he's mixed"). People assume that racial categories are biological, and therefore fixed; but the fact that they can change from black to mixed reveals them to be social classifications.

In Brazil, Obama would most likely be called *mulato*, but not because his father was African and his mother traced her ancestry to Europe. Although Americans categorize people racially by ancestry, Brazilians do so by what they look like. Obama simply doesn't look African enough to Brazilian eyes to be called *preto* or *negro*.

Is Obama African American? If the question means, "Does he identify with and is he accepted as a member of this group?" the answer is "Yes." But if it means, "Is he descended from slaves in the United States?" the answer is "No."* Furthermore, since nearly all American slaves came from West Africa, and Kenya is in East Africa, Obama doesn't even share a regional ancestry with African Americans.

Census categories are the product of politicians rather than scientists (though scientists play a role in tidying up the conceptual disarray handed to them). Over the decades—as we have gone from slavery to segregation to desegregation to some degree of integration—legal definitions of race have changed. In the 2010 census, Barack Obama was free to choose among *black, black and white,* or even conceivably *white.* Leaving these options open to the individual shows a degree of recognition that race is a social rather than biological category, since Obama would not have been free to choose his sex from among male, male and female, or even conceivably female (in recognition of the larger size of the X chromosome).

Barack Obama is what he is. We know what he looks like; we know about his parents and ancestry. The question "Is Barack Obama black or mixed?" appears to ask for information about him, but in fact it gives clues to the cultural categories Americans use in thinking about "race."

What Are You?

American tourists in Norway may occasionally come across Sami (they prefer not to be called Lapps) or have locals call attention to them and their brightly colored clothes. If there is an opportunity for small talk, one of the first questions

---

*As this book was going to press, genealogy research by Ancestry.com argued that Barack Obama's mother's eleventh great-grandfather was probably John Punch, one of the first African slaves in America.

probably would be, "How many reindeer do you have?" The question might be a way of showing interest by referring to a well-known fact, as in "Brazil-Carnival," "Sami-reindeer." It is an innocent question, perhaps stemming from the Golden Rule—Do unto others as you would have others do unto you—since, if the tourists owned any reindeer, they would be glad to tell you how many. To the Sami, however, the question is impertinent. It is like asking Americans how much money they have in the bank.

In every culture there is certain information that people feel they need in order to interact with one another, and other information that is accepted as private. In the United States, probably because of our history of complex and often tense race relations, Americans feel they need to know one another's race in order to modulate their behavior. Most Americans are easy to label—they look "white," "black," or (East) "Asian," and speak a recognizable dialect of American English. But a large (and growing) number of individuals do not fit easily into one of these categories. Ambiguity arises because in the United States we classify people racially, based on ancestry (or "blood"), and not merely by first impressions of their appearance.

As in the United States, Brazil also has a long history of slavery, discrimination, and complex race relations; but Brazilians don't share our need to categorize ambiguous-looking people. The reason is that their racial classifications in terms of *tipos* are based on what people look like, not their ancestry. For example, a family in Salvador, Bahia, of two parents and six children might be eight different *tipos*. When you know someone's *tipo*, you know more or less what they look like (but not their ancestors' *tipos*)—so there is no ambiguity to be clarified.

Here is a possible, condensed conversation between a white American man and an accent-free American woman with light, tan skin; black, wavy hair; brown eyes; a nose that is neither narrow nor broad; and lips that are neither thin nor thick:

"What is your name?"

"Jennifer Smith."

"What is your mother's name?"

"Mary Jones."

"Where were your parents born?"

"Here."

"What language did you speak at home?"

"English."

What is going on in this interaction?

He wants to know her race and believes he is entitled to that information. He has probably ruled out Asian and South Asian but is still trying to decide among white, black, Latino, or in some parts of the country, Native American. He may be feeling frustrated or wonder why she hasn't caught his drift.

She knows what she looks like, what her ancestry and cultural background are, and understands the question he really wants answered: "What are you?" That is, "Do you have any black or Latino ancestry?" But she finds the interaction intrusive—a bit like a Sami man being asked, "How many reindeer do you have?"

Is it really essential to know other people's race? Maybe we should reformulate the Golden Rule to take cultural differences into account: Do unto others as they would have done unto them.

How People Change Their Ethnicity

The number of Native Americans has been increasing faster than can be accounted for by the birth rate. Sound impossible? This is just one of many surprises that emerge when you look at ethnicity up close. The main explanation is probably the emergence of casinos on reservations. It would seem that, as some impoverished tribes have grown rich, many people have been "rediscovering their roots" and labeling themselves accordingly. As we Americans say, "Money talks."

Brazilians say, "Money whitens." In Brazil there are numerous "racial" terms, blurring into one another, that describe what people look like. As a result, as people become more affluent they think of themselves as whiter, refer to themselves with whiter terminology, and may even be described by others as whiter. For example, here is a Brazilian joke from the 1970s about the soccer superstar Pelé:

> A mother sees her tan-skinned daughter holding hands with a much darker man. She frowns and asks her friend, "Who is that man?" The woman tells her excitedly, "That's Pelé!" "Oh," the mother smiles, "I didn't know she was going out with a white man."

As with Native Americans, the number of Irish Americans exceeds calculations from births and immigration, even though there are no Irish casinos. In this case, the explanation can be found in our kinship system and the tendency of people to marry within their religion. Among Roman Catholics in our predominantly Protestant former British colony, the English-speaking Irish are the most prestigious group. Thus, if Mr. Murphy marries Ms. Garcia or Ms. Kowalski, all their children take the name Murphy and have the option of adopting an Irish ethnicity. This is not true if the genders are reversed, and Mr. Garcia or Mr. Kowalski marries Ms. Murphy.

A group can also seem smaller than its numbers. Many people assume that the English, or at least the British—which includes the Irish, Scots, and Welch—are our largest white ethnic group. This is not the case, however; German Americans are the most numerous—more than all the British Americans combined. Think of our all-American foods: the hamburger (from Hamburg) and the frankfurter (from Frankfurt), also known as the wiener (from Vienna, which is *Wien* in German). The Holocaust and two world wars with Germany have stigmatized this group, so that many people of German descent avoid an ethnic label and choose instead to blend in with the undifferentiated mass of white Americans. Consider McDonald's hamburgers—transformed from the German original by a Scottish/Irish brand name—or our presidents Hoover and Eisenhower whom we rarely associate with German descent.

Both race (which many Americans consider a biological category) and ethnicity (which many consider cultural) are cultural concepts; but in America we seem to view ethnicity as more or less malleable, while race is fixed. We seem to think of ethnicity as socially learned, but race as biologically inherited. If a German American acts like a British American, that is no big deal compared to someone who is "really black" "passing for white." Matters are different in other cultures. In Brazil, that person would be "really white," and in any event adjusting one's race from time to time is not a matter of great consequence.

How to Change Your Race

It doesn't sound possible. We Americans believe that race is a biological given, something you are born with and that you can't change; but we are wrong. And an avocado can show us the way.

The avocado is a vegetable that we eat in salad with oil and vinegar—or, borrowing from Mexico, mashed up with tomatoes and spices in guacamole. In Brazil, however, the avocado is a fruit; people eat it for dessert with lemon juice and sugar.

Anthropologists call the ways a culture classifies things *folk taxonomies*. The Brazilian folk taxonomy for edible plants classifies the avocado as a fruit, while the American one does not. Botanists would also say that it is a fruit—but this does not mean that Brazilians are right and Americans are wrong. It just means that in Portuguese the scientific meaning and the folk meaning are represented by the same word, *fruta*, while English has two different words, *fruit* and *vegetable*.

This example also illustrates the general problem involved in translating languages and cultural concepts. Portuguese-English dictionaries will translate *fruta* as *fruit*, and vice versa; but we can see that the meanings are not identical, since *fruta* includes avocados and *fruit* does not.

Just as botanical folk taxonomies classify edible plants, racial folk taxonomies classify people. And different cultures have different racial folk taxonomies.

The American folk taxonomy of race is based on ancestry (called *blood*). According to the "one drop rule," if one or both parents are black, then all the children are black, regardless of what they look like. Also, all of a couple's children are of the same race.

The Brazilian folk taxonomy of race has a huge number of categories, called *tipos*, based on visible traits such as skin color, hair color and form, eye color, and facial features. In the United States, I am white, and the other five members of my family—my wife, daughter, son-in-law, and two grandchildren—are black. In Brazil, we are six different *tipos*.

I was once walking in a park in São Paulo, and a man who probably recognized my clothes as foreign asked where I was from. When I said, "The United States," he said, "Here we call people who look like you *turcos*." I have no Turkish ancestry, but of course that is an amusing tidbit, irrelevant to my *tipo*.

If my family and I were to take some avocados with us on a flight from New York to Rio de Janeiro, the avocados would change from vegetables to fruits, and we would change from two races to six *tipos*. The change is not in what the six of us (or the avocados) look like, or our genes, or ancestry. It is in the culture-specific concepts used to classify people and edible plants.

So the way to change your race is to go to a place with a racial folk taxonomy that classifies you differently.

CHAPTER 3

Racial Myths and Cultural Misunderstandings

The sections of this chapter examine a variety of confusions, misinterpretations, and awkward encounters that result from mixing biological assumptions about race with cultural assumptions. The discussions point up lessons we can learn from such misunderstandings.

How Come Other Folks All Look Alike?

Nearly twenty-five years ago I was having dinner at a restaurant in Jakarta, Indonesia, with a group of psychologists from various countries. Only two of us were men, and we were both white Americans. The other man was several inches taller than I, significantly heavier, and had lighter-colored hair— though we both wore glasses and had short beards. Despite the (to me) obvious contrast in our appearance, the waiter kept getting our orders mixed up; and it became evident that he couldn't tell the difference between us.

The waiter's difficulty represents a fairly general perceptual phenomenon. For example, I would sometimes ask students in my cross-cultural psychology class, "Who are more varied in what they look like, whites or blacks?" Among those who felt secure enough to raise their hands, whites said that whites are more varied, and blacks said that blacks are more varied.

Visual perception begins developing in infancy. In general, white babies and children see more white faces and learn to make the fine distinctions necessary to tell who is who, and black babies and children see more black faces and learn comparable visual distinctions.

One of the byproducts of organizing marriage, neighborhoods, and other social categories along color lines is the development of a kind of perceptual provinciality within each group. Early in my marriage, I would sometimes ask my African American wife, "Is so-and-so black?" I have become more accurate over the years but have by no means fully compensated for my early perceptual training.

Psychologists have shown that there are many problems with eyewitness testimony. These difficulties are compounded when a victim has to identify the face of a perpetrator of a different race who was seen only fleetingly during a traumatic event.

Apart from people's perceptual learning, there is an objective answer to the question of whether whites or blacks are more varied in what they look like. In fact, blacks are more diverse in appearance, as is evident to outsiders to the American experience. A woman who was an immigrant from the Philippines told me just this: "Blacks are more varied."

Why is this so? The cultural answer comes from America's one-drop rule—anyone with "black blood" is black. It is a strange rule. It means that a white woman can give birth to a black baby—for example our president—but a black woman cannot give birth to a white baby. The latter might be white in

Brazil and would be classified in various ways in other cultures. But if children of a black mother in the United States said they were white, they would be merely pretending—"passing for white."

The one-drop rule explains why there are light-skinned blacks and dark-skinned blacks, but only light-skinned whites (even though, for reasons of perceptual learning, whites are aware of skin color variations among themselves). If we had a different cultural rule—for example, anyone with "white blood" is white—then the race of many American blacks would change, and whites would become more varied in appearance.

What Does It Mean to Look Jewish?

A number of years ago, I was walking down the street near my house; and a man I had never seen before stopped me and said, "Hiya Rabbi! I haven't seen you since the wedding."

As you may have guessed, I am not a rabbi.

I have been to Germany on a number of extended visits—getting to know the language, people, and culture—and several times, as part of showing me around, friendly individuals have pointed out less-than-obvious local Holocaust memorials. (For example, commemorative plaques on walls, or a train station near a park we were visiting from which Jews had been shipped off to Auschwitz.) My ethnic identity or religious beliefs were never discussed, but I wonder whether these sights would have been pointed out to me if I looked different.

Assimilated European-American Jews—who eschew distinctive clothing, headgear, hairstyles, and food preferences—have been able to blend in to the American mainstream for at least several decades. They think of themselves as no different from anyone else—that is, as "white"—and not as recognizably "other."

It was not always this way. A little over a century ago, when my grandparents arrived at Ellis Island as part of the wave of immigration from Eastern Europe, most Americans viewed them not as "white," but as part of a "Jewish race."

Even now, vestiges of that cultural belief remain in the concept of "Jewish blood." An atheist whose parents are Jewish is still believed by many to have Jewish blood—in much the same way that a white-appearing child of at least one black parent is believed to have black blood. In contrast, a person born to Christian parents who converts to Judaism is believed not to have Jewish blood—nor is there a folk concept of "Christian blood." Americans, especially Jewish Americans, may avoid the word "blood"—but most Jews and non-Jews alike share a belief that there is some Jewish essence that parents pass down to their children, but which converts do not possess.

(There is, in fact, something important about Jewishness that is passed down from parents to children. It just isn't Eastern European facial features or a pseudo-biological entity called "blood." It is culture.)

So, when many American Jews find themselves being treated differently from other whites because of what they look like (even when the behavior is well-intentioned, as with my German acquaintances) they get upset. This is because their illusion that they are "just like everyone else" has been challenged.

African Americans and other non-whites born in the United States do not grow up with that illusion, because they are "visible minorities." From early childhood, they learn that they look different from the majority, and they know that whites see them that way. So they are not comparably disconcerted when even well-intentioned whites act in ways based on the assumption of difference.

What Do Names Tell Us About Race and Religion?

Names communicate a lot of information, which is subject to both interpretation and misinterpretation. This includes information about race and religion; and, when you think about it, inferences about race and religion are actually inferences about culture. For example, in addition to communicating "Italian," the surname Bianchi also communicates "Roman Catholic" and "white." (Bianchi even means "white.")

Here are four surnames: Chan, Garcia, Obama, Patel. In terms of American folk categories of race, they respectively convey the information Asian, Latino, black, and . . . what? As I indicated in the last chapter, Americans haven't yet reached a cultural consensus on the racial categorization of South Asians. So, on hearing someone referred to as Mr. Patel, most Americans would guess what race he is *not* (white), and might presume that he has Indian ancestry, but wouldn't have a handy answer for what race he *is*.

Here are three more surnames: Christian, Cohen, Mohammed. To most Americans, these names convey the religious information Christian, Jewish, Muslim. By law, in the United States, freedom of religion is an individual right guaranteed by the First Amendment. So an individual with any of these last names could be a member of any of the three religions, or of any other religion, or of no religion.

Consider the case of former Secretary of Defense William Cohen—he is a Christian. As his last name suggests, his father was Jewish (though his mother was not). Since Judaism is passed down through the maternal line, in addition to his choice not to be Jewish, Jewish religious tradition also deems him not to be Jewish. Still, most Americans would say that he has "Jewish blood," suggesting a racial dimension to Jewishness not present in Christianness.

As with other cultural information conveyed by last names, racial and religious inferences only apply to a person's father (or father's father, or someone further back in the male line). And, as with other cultural information, one can examine the relationship between given names and surnames for consistency or contrast of information.

Here are two sets of women's names: (1) Mai Chan, Maria Garcia, Latoya Obama, Indira Patel, and Grace Christian, Rebecca Cohen, Aisha Mohammed; and (2) Isabella Chan, Abigail Garcia, Madison Obama, Sophia Patel, and Olivia Christian, Mia Cohen, Chloe Mohammed. The first set contains given names that are consistent with the racial or religious information suggested by the family names; and the second set contains given names from the ten most popular in 2010. (As an exercise, try making up two comparable sets of men's names.)

The first set of names would seem to communicate the parents' desire to emphasize the racial or religious information conveyed by the family name, while the second set would downplay that in favor of a generalized Americanness. As children grow into adults, their racial or religious identities may turn out to be important to them—or not very important; and so their names may or may not present issues for them to grapple with. For example, a person with a religious name who has chosen a different religion, or is an agnostic or atheist, would be confronted with a problem not faced by a devout follower of his or her parents' religion.

Thus, the ways individuals react to the racial or religious information conveyed by the names they received—living up to it, ignoring it, or rebelling against it—helps us to understand how they see themselves and their place in the world.

How Should Racism Be Defined?

When my granddaughter was little, she came to me with a new insight.

"Do you know why they call it lasagna?" she asked.

"No. Why?"

"Because it looks like lasagna!"

What makes this example so charming is the belief that words are related to the concepts they represent in some essential way—that there is a lasagna-ness in the word *lasagna* that makes it the best name for the food. Of course, this is incorrect. Words are just a bunch of sounds. There is no apple-ness in the word apple, since *maçã* works just fine in Portuguese, as do *pomme* in French and other words in other languages.

The word *racism* is now used in a variety of ways, but substituting other words for each meaning and employing it in a particular anthropological sense can clarify matters and make for greater precision—like distinguishing lasagna from spaghetti or macaroni.

Words may change their meanings over time or depending on context. *Personality* used to refer to one's artificial social exterior (*persona* means mask in Latin); now it refers to what a person is really like. *Racism* changes its meaning too, depending on how people use it in a given context—whether to refer to hostile acts, antagonistic emotions, negative attitudes, or specific beliefs. Distinguishing among some common meanings of racism allows us to avoid vagueness by using more precise terms.

One meaning is holding pre-formed negative opinions or stereotypes about a group or category of people. *Prejudice* (from pre-judging) and *bigotry* are good words for that concept.

Another meaning is treating people badly or unfairly because of their group membership or social classification. This involves actions stemming from prejudice, as opposed to passively holding biased beliefs, hiding negative emotions, or minimizing contact with those in disliked categories. *Discrimination* expresses that concept well.

I would argue for a particular anthropological definition, even though it may seem strange on first view—*racism is the belief that culture is inherited.* That is, it is a belief that groups of people behave in distinctive ways not because they have learned to do so, but because their members share some inherited essence (called "blood"; or sometimes "genes"—but without reference to specific DNA sequences).

Here are two examples of racism by this anthropological definition:

The belief that blacks are inherently superior basketball players. Actually, tall, muscular, well-coordinated, competitive people who practice a lot make good basketball players. The Mbuti pygmies in Africa would be at a disadvantage on the basketball court.

The belief that Eastern European Jews and Asians are inherently more intelligent than others. Cultures that place a strong emphasis on formal education and that use a variety of rewards, punishments, and exposure to academic and intellectual activities and role models excel at promoting their children's cognitive development. Hmong children in the United States lag in school performance, because, although Asian, they lack the cultural emphasis on education.

The anthropological definition helps us to identify pseudo-biological explanations for cultural differences as the distinguishing feature of racism. Focusing our attention on pseudo-biological explanations prevents us from confusing racism with other forms of bad behavior.

Cultural Misunderstandings

At a psychology conference in England years ago, a woman said to me, "I'll knock you up in the morning." I was initially taken aback by her bizarre suggestion, but it did occur to me that I might not understand her intent. Eventually, it turned out that what she meant was, "I'll knock on your door in the morning so that we can meet for breakfast to discuss the panel we're on."

This example, of a dialect difference in the meaning of "knock you up" between British and American English, illustrates the complications that can arise from a cultural misunderstanding. A cultural misunderstanding occurs when something—a word, gesture, object, social context, almost anything you can think of—has different meanings in two cultures. Sometimes the misunderstandings get resolved, sometimes they lead nowhere, and sometimes they can escalate to anything from love to war.

Consider the Latin lover. It is not a concept you come across in Latin America. It seems to be an American stereotype—perhaps shared by some other non-Latin cultures. One possible origin of the concept is in a cultural misunderstanding regarding personal space. While there are variations throughout Latin America, and in the United States as well, in general, Latin Americans stand closer to one another when speaking than do Americans. When a Latin American man is talking to an American woman, from her point of view he is entering her personal space. There are several reasons an American man might do so, one of which is erotic interest. If she finds him attractive and interprets his proximity as a sign of interest—even though he had no such intent—she may reciprocate. Cultures differ in how men respond to unsolicited expressions of interest from a woman, and machismo varies from place to place in Latin America, but in general it is quite likely that the man will respond in turn, leading to an escalation of sexual interest, and providing "evidence" for the Latin lover stereotype.

Race is another area where cultural misunderstandings are common. Because we Americans tend to assume that racial categories are biological rather than social, it may not occur to us that people from other cultures have a different set of racial concepts and classify themselves and us differently. For example, some African Americans complain that certain immigrants from other countries—such as Haiti or Jamaica—"act as if they aren't black." The cultural misunderstanding is that, in the immigrants' countries of origin, they may well not be black. But that doesn't mean that they think they are white. It just means that their cultures have more categories—like *marabou* or *grimaud* in Haiti, or *fair* or *brown* in Jamaica—than are used in the United States. Meanwhile, American whites, unaware of the cultural diversity, might blithely assume that the immigrants are black, without even realizing that an issue existed.

Resolving cultural misunderstandings can clear the air, or even lead to laughter. Sometimes, though, when it comes to race, unidentified cultural misunderstandings can also lead to festering resentments.

Was Brazil's President Lula Racially Insensitive to President Obama?

At the 2009 summit of the G-20 in London, Brazil's President Lula (Luiz Inacio da Silva) said of our president, "I am a fan of Obama. He is the first US president who has our face. If you ran into him in Bahia, you would think he's from there." This comment seemed insensitive to some Americans, who heard it as, "We have blacks like you in Bahia."

I used to teach psychology in Brazil, and I have heard such comments before. When an American interracial couple was at a party in São Paulo, a Brazilian anthropologist (with a British doctorate) who was chatting with them said to the black husband, "We have a lot of people who look like you in Bahia." Anthropology is the discipline most knowledgeable about race and most sensitive to it, so the remark—made in a friendly tone and in all innocence—is a reminder that there is no escape from culture. Brazilian anthropologists are culturally Brazilian and may unintentionally offend Americans (and American anthropologists are culturally American and may show similar inadvertent insensitivity to Brazilians).

Salvador, the capital of the state of Bahia (and the first capital of Brazil), is often referred to simply as Bahia. West African influences are omnipresent there, especially in the food, music, and religion. When African dignitaries visit the country, they are often brought to Bahia to show them how much like home life in the city appears. Brazilians view it as a predominantly black city with an easygoing tropical life style. The character of this port city can be traced back to its history as the center of the Brazilian slave trade. Slavery in Brazil was much more widespread than in the United States and came to an end only in 1888, after it had been abolished in the rest of the New World.

Unlike the United States, where our concept of race is based on ancestry (called blood), Brazil's concept of race (*tipo*) is based on appearance. Your race is what you look like, regardless of what your parents, relatives, or ancestors look like—and numerous descriptive terms are used. Thus, Brazilians say that one of the proofs that Americans are racist is that we call people black who aren't black. (Brazilian racism is indicated in their assumption that darker is less desirable, so that it is derogatory to call someone black who has tan skin, or wavy hair, or blue eyes, or simply has a lot of money.)

While race is a fraught topic for Americans, Brazilians are more comfortable and even playful in talking about it. For example, when I didn't recognize the name of one of my students, a secretary referred to him as *"aquele queimadinho"*—"that slightly burned-looking guy."

Brazilians also tend to assume they are of mixed background. During one poor people's Carnival on the outskirts of the city of Campinas, I watched a Samba School called *Miscegenation*. They had three floats, representing Europeans, Africans, and Native Brazilians—and their message was one of pride in mixed ancestry.

Without an understanding of the meaning of Bahia to Brazilians, Lula's comment might sound both offensive and a bit bizarre—as if a white American president were to say of an Afro-Brazilian president, "I am a fan of his. He is the first Brazilian president who has our face. If you ran into him in Mississippi, you would think he's from there."

Lula might have meant to convey something like, "Afro-Bahians are warm, informal, and friendly; and Obama in his resemblance to their looks and personality feels like one of us."

Harry Potter and the Racial Misunderstanding

A number of years ago, while I was struggling to learn German, I hit on the idea of reading *Harry Potter and the Sorcerer's Stone* in German. The book was so popular I knew I could find a German edition, and the sentences were sure to be shorter and the vocabulary easier than in most translated novels. By keeping the English version open alongside the German, I wouldn't have to stop every few words to look in a bilingual dictionary.

I labored through half a dozen chapters with more difficulty than a fourth grader, until I was brought up short by a missing sentence. "'Thomas, Dean,' a Black boy even taller than Ron, joined Harry at the Gryffindor table" was on page 122 in English, but it didn't exist in the German edition.

What could this possibly mean? I thought back on the book and couldn't remember any black characters. Was the point of the deletion to make Hogwarts into an all-white school in deference to German readers? I didn't want to believe it, given all the changes in Germany since World War II and the country's atonement for its Nazi past. But what other possible explanation could there be?

I wrote to J. K. Rowling's literary agent to inquire, and eventually wound up with the following explanation. I assumed I had been reading the English language version, but actually I had been reading the American edition. There was also a British edition with a different title—*Harry Potter and the Sorcerer's Stone* in the United States was *Harry Potter and the Philosopher's Stone* in the United Kingdom. The sentence in question had been deleted by the British publisher in a space-saving edit; and the German edition was a translation of the British edition. In other words, the German translator had not deleted the sentence. He had never even seen it.

The moral of the story is that the world is a complicated place, and it is difficult to know why things happen or what people's motivations are. It is a good idea to remain open to non-racial explanations for apparently racially charged occurrences.

You can look it up in the Hogwarts curriculum.

CHAPTER 4

Racial Myths in the Census

The kinds of confusions about race discussed in the last chapter are evident in the census. Although the 2010 census is behind us, its problematic racial classifications left many questions about science, politics, and American culture unanswered. This chapter travels through time in the United States—from the first census to the most recent—and across space to Brazil's 2010 census, to examine just how unstable census race categories are, and what that means for understanding the race concept. It also proposes a way that the American census could gather needed information without confusing people or contradicting science.

Problems With the Census Race Categories

As was discussed in previous chapters, there is a longstanding consensus among scientific specialists—evolutionary biologists and biological anthropologists—that the human species has no races in the biological sense. What people look like and people's genes vary gradually around the planet, with the great majority of variation in Africa where our species originated, and where humans have lived the longest. If humans did have biological races, they would all be in Africa.

There is also a cultural concept of race. This concept varies from culture to culture and changes over time within any given culture. In the United States, factors such as the ends of slavery and of segregation, waves of immigration from various parts of the world, and patterns of intermarriage have all contributed to changing Americans' cultural concept of race in the past, and can be expected to do so in the future.

The government needs the census to count the population and collect statistics about various legally defined groups, so that appropriations can be properly distributed. However, in the 2010 Census questions eight and nine needlessly muddled the cultural and biological race concepts. In addition, they asked individuals to choose among cultural categories that do not correspond to common usage—thereby unnecessarily antagonizing or perplexing many people. For example, if asked to list races, most Americans would offer some variant of the terms *white, black,* and *Asian*—perhaps adding *American Indian* and/or *Latino.* (They might even include *Arab*—a term missing from the Census.) In contrast, the Census listed fifteen races but excluded Latino. Most Americans would agree that discrimination against Latinos is a form of racial discrimination. But by separating question eight about Latinos from question nine about race, thereby insisting that Latinos are not a race, the Census needlessly contradicted cultural assumptions.

The following detailed presentation of questions eight and nine makes clear the problems they create. Question eight asks if you are of Hispanic, Latino, or Spanish origin, and makes you choose one of the following options: (1) No; (2) Yes, Mexican, Mexican American, Chicano; (3) Yes, Puerto Rican; (4)

Yes, Cuban; (5) Yes, another Hispanic, Latino, or Spanish origin (and leaves a space for you to write in the term).

Question nine asks your race and allows you to check one or more of the following races: (1) White; (2) Black, African American, or Negro; (3) American Indian or Alaskan Native (and leaves a space for you to write in your enrolled or principal tribe); (4) Asian Indian; (5) Chinese; (6) Filipino; (7) Japanese; (8) Korean; (9) Vietnamese; (10) Other Asian (and leaves a space for you to write in your race); (11) Native Hawaiian; (12) Guamanian or Chamorro; (13) Samoan; (14) Other Pacific Islander (and leaves a space for you to write in your race); and (15) Some other race (and leaves a space for you to write in your race).

One might ask, "Why these, and only these races, and not others?" And why does question nine not allow an option of "No race"—the only biologically correct answer?

The Census needlessly offends many Americans by asking them their race. Furthermore, a large percentage of respondents—mainly, but not exclusively, Latinos—found question nine confusing. They often checked "some other race," as they did in 2000; and many filled in the box with terms from question eight, such as "Mexican American" or "Hispanic." This creates unnecessary problems in analyzing the data.

There is a better and simpler way to collect the needed information. It maintains the census's terminology and avoids unnecessarily introducing the confusion about race. All that is needed is to combine all the descriptive terms in questions eight and nine into a single question and ask, "Which of the following terms describe you? (Check as many as apply.)"

Avoiding the pseudo-biological word *race*, and replacing it with the neutral descriptor *term* clears away the confusion with no loss of information.

This simple solution would allow the government to obtain the numbers it needs for the categories it wants to count, and allows individuals to choose the terms they prefer to describe themselves. It also avoids putting the government in the position of making people choose their race when scientists agree that races don't exist.

Slavery

American culture at the time of the 2010 census had changed greatly since the first census in 1790. The Constitution calls for a census every ten years; and this section begins at the beginning by considering the race categories in the first eight of the twenty-three censuses. During the period 1790 to 1860 slavery was institutionalized in the United States.

The government's 2010 official census website justified asking individuals to list their race by saying that the question has been "Asked since 1790." This is not an accurate statement.

In fact, the term "race" didn't appear on the census until 1900, and with the exception of 1950 it has been the sole descriptor (as opposed to "color or race") for a census item only since 1990. This is scientifically bizarre.

In 1941 the anthropologist Ashley Montagu first proposed that the human species had no races in the biological sense; by the 1960s this was the dominant view in physical anthropology and evolutionary biology; and it has been the consensus view in those fields for decades. Scientists now agree that all that exists is gradual variability in what people look like, and in their genetic makeup, as one travels around the planet. In other words, while scientific knowledge has been moving away from race, census terminology has been reifying it.

The first census in 1790 had only six questions, and counted males and females as free whites, other free persons, and slaves. From then until 1860—the last census before the Civil War—these were more or less the categories used, though the number of questions asked on the census increased from six to twenty-three. The additional questions were aimed at getting information about age, occupation, and other characteristics such as "whether deaf and dumb, blind, insane, idiotic, pauper, or convict." They also asked about the number of slaves that were fugitives, the number manumitted (freed), and the number of slave houses.

The term *color*—not *race*—first appeared in the 1850 census, with three options: white, black, or mulatto; and these options were repeated in 1860. Whatever folk beliefs about "race" Americans may have held prior to the Civil War, they were of secondary importance. Instead, the census questions were organized around the institution of slavery, and were aimed at getting the information needed to apportion taxes and allocate congressional representation.

The key to understanding these questions is political, not biological. The Three-Fifths Compromise was the deal that made possible the formation of a national government consisting of both free states and slave states; and it did so by counting each slave as three-fifths of a person. (The constitution euphemistically avoided the words "slave" or "slavery" by referring to "other Persons.") The interrelatedness of the three critical issues of congressional representation, the distribution of taxes, and the creation of the census is embodied in the way they are bound together in just two sentences. Here is the relevant part of Article 1, Section 2, Paragraph 3 of the United States Constitution:

Representatives and direct Taxes shall be apportioned among the several States which may be included within this Union, according to their respective Numbers, which shall be determined by adding to the whole Number of free Persons, including those bound to Service for a Term of Years, and excluding Indians not taxed, three fifths of all other Persons. The actual Enumeration shall be made within three Years after the first Meeting of the Congress of the United States, and within every subsequent Term of ten Years, in such Manner as they shall by Law direct.

After the Civil War, the 14th Amendment changed this section.

Jim Crow

This section continues looking at the changes in the census race questions over time by considering the period from Reconstruction through the Great Depression.

The American Civil War took place from 1861 to 1865, and with its end the need to count the slave population disappeared. Census terminology did, however, retain the "color" category, and the 1870 census added two additional colors—Chinese and Indian. These same five colors were repeated in 1880, and the 1890 census added another three colors—quadroon, octoroon, and Japanese.

The terms *mulatto*, *quadroon*, and *octoroon* reify the nonscientific American folk concept of blood. Blood is a biological entity, and many people inaccurately believe that it is the same as genes. The following explanation shows why they are wrong.

Suppose that there are eight genes for race, so that a mulatto has four black genes and four white genes, a quadroon has two black genes and six white genes, and an octoroon has one black gene and seven white genes. Now suppose that a mulatto man and a mulatto woman have a lot of children. Each child would get half its genes from the father and half from the mother. One child might get all four white genes from each parent and be 100 percent white, another might get all four black genes from each parent and be 100 percent black, and other children might wind up with all the other possible combinations of white and black genes. However, American culture views mulattos as black (e.g., President Obama), and believes that two blacks cannot have a 100 percent white baby. This is why the folk concept of blood does not act like genes.

Blood is actually another word for *ancestry*. *Mulatto* is an American cultural term for someone with one parent who is culturally classified as black; *quadroon* is an American cultural term for someone with one grandparent who is culturally classified as black; and *octoroon* is an American cultural term for someone with one great-grandparent who is culturally classified as black (or two great-great-grandparents, etc.).

Although biological races do not exist, folk beliefs like these about why people look different from one another have long been with us. As the census tried to make the folk beliefs countable, inadequacies of classification appeared, and the categories proliferated. The expansion from three to eight colors in the latter half of the nineteenth century is evident once again in the 2010 census, which lists fifteen races. At the same time, problems with classification open the door to ever more categories. The current census excludes "Latino" and similar terms from its list of races, even though many Americans would disagree. We know that many Americans self-classified as "other" on the 2010 census and wrote in a term such as "Mexican" for their race. Furthermore, additional cultural terms, such as "Arab," do not appear at all. Conscientious participants can be excused for their perplexity at wondering why Korean and Vietnamese are two different races, but neither Puerto Rican nor Cuban is a race.

The censuses from 1900 to 1940 solved the category proliferation problem by allowing the individual to write in a descriptor. At the same time, however, the preexisting color category became "color or race." This took place at a time when Jim Crow laws enforced segregation and other laws prohibited interracial marriage in the South, while de facto segregation was the norm in the North. Many people were sterilized (with blacks greatly overrepresented) as the eugenics movement sought to breed intellectually superior Americans. In other words, the introduction of the term "race" to the census emphasized the de facto and de jure segregation and the scientific racism of that period.

Civil Rights and the Cold War

The end of de jure segregation and racial discrimination led to changes in American culture that were accompanied by changes in the "racial" categories and concepts used by the census. (In order to simplify the discussion, extended descriptions of some of the changes are listed in footnotes.)

The 1950 census was the first to use the term "race" as the sole descriptor. "Race" had appeared in the census for the first time in 1900 as part of the category "color or race"—terminology that continued through 1940. The 1950 census specified seven races: White, Negro, American Indian, Japanese, Chinese, Filipino, and Other race (spell out).

A comparison with the eight options of the 1890 census sixty years earlier shows that only three descriptors were identical (White, Japanese, and Chinese). Terms such as *mulatto*, *quadroon*, and *octoroon* had long since disappeared. Sixty years later, in 2010, with "race" once again as the sole descriptor, and with fifteen options, these are also the only three identical terms. (We know from research on psychological testing and polling that slight changes in wording can lead to dramatic changes in responses, so that, for example, "Indian" and "American Indian" on different censuses cannot be considered to be the same descriptor.)

The dramatic changes in "racial" classifications over time are clear evidence that they are cultural categories rather than biological ones, and that their use in the census has resulted from political decisions rather than scientific evidence.

In 1960 the term "race" disappeared from the census and was replaced by "Is this person—White, Negro, American Indian, Japanese, Chinese, Filipino, Hawaiian, Part Hawaiian, Aleut, Eskimo, (etc.)?" Eliminating the term "race" when collecting needed information—as I suggested above—has long been advocated by anthropologists and other specialists. However, at the same time as implementing this desirable practice, the 1960 census once again proliferated categories by adding four new ones. In addition, the question implied that individuals could only choose one term. A response of "White, Negro, and American Indian" would seem to contradict the instructions, even though many people might think of themselves that way.

The 1970 census made a series of changes.* These included reintroducing the category "color or race" and increasing the number of options to nine. In an odd move, Aleut and Eskimo were races only in Alaska, and Hawaiian and Korean were races everywhere except Alaska. Thus, Americans could change their race by moving to or from Alaska; and the actual number of races counted by the census was eleven. In addition, for the first time the census created a separate question about Latin American "origin or descent."

The 1980 census once again allowed individuals to choose only one descriptor.** However, it returned to the "Is this person" format—eliminating the word "race"—and expanding the number of options to fifteen. It also continued the practice of using a separate question for "Spanish/Hispanic origin or descent."

---

*These are the changes: (1) Question four reintroduced the category "color or race"; (2) the term "Part Hawaiian" was eliminated; (3) individuals were explicitly made to choose only one term; (4) for Hawaii and the forty-eight contiguous states the number of options increased to nine: White, Negro, Indian (Amer.) Print tribe____, Japanese, Chinese, Filipino, Hawaiian, Korean, Other—Print race _____; for Alaska, the categories "Aleut" and "Eskimo" were substituted for "Hawaiian" and "Korean"—thus, the total number of options was actually eleven; and (5) in addition, question 13-b. requested information clearly labeled as different from color or race—"Is this person's origin or descent" and gave six options—Mexican, Puerto Rican, Cuban, Central or South American, Other Spanish, and No, none of these.

**In reinstituting the practice of allowing individuals to choose only one descriptor, the 1980 census returned to the "Is this person" format—eliminating the word "race"—and expanding the number of options to fifteen: White, Black or Negro, Japanese, Chinese, Filipino, Korean, Vietnamese, Asian Indian, Hawaiian, Guamanian, Samoan, Eskimo, Aleut, Indian (Amer.) Print tribe _____, Other—Specify ____. As in 1970, a separate question was created for Latinos. This time it was worded, "Is this person of Spanish/Hispanic origin or descent?" and gave five options: No (not Spanish/Hispanic); Yes, Mexican, Mexican-Amer., Chicano; Yes, Puerto Rican; Yes, Cuban; Yes, other Spanish/Hispanic.

The on-again-off-again nature of the "Is this person" format began in 1960, around the time that scientists reached a consensus that *race* was not a biological concept applicable to the human species. Since the designers of the census have long been aware of the scientific facts, it is reasonable to interpret the oscillation as resulting from the conflict between scientific knowledge and political considerations. Not surprisingly, political considerations appear to have won, since the term "race"—not even "color or race"—has been used as the exclusive descriptor since 1990.

A second kind of distinction began in the 1970 census. This was to separate Latin American descent (not called "race") from other kinds of descent ("race"). For example, a large proportion of the "octoroons" of the 1890 census could have "passed for white." They would in fact have been considered white (or *fair* or *blanco* or *branco* or *blanc*) throughout Latin America and the Caribbean, but not in the United States, because they had "black blood"—that is, African descent. In contrast, most Americans would consider Latinos a race and discrimination against them racial discrimination, but the census refuses to acknowledge this cultural classification.

In short, science says that neither whites nor blacks nor Latinos are a race; American culture says that all three are races; and contradicting both, the census says that whites and blacks are races but that Latinos are not.

Recent Censuses

This section brings us up to date. I have included a fair amount of detail at the outset because the most recent censuses contain the politically created categories we are now living with.

The 1990 census, as well as the two subsequent ones, used only the term "race"—thereby insisting on this category definition. It allowed individuals to choose only one of six races: White, Black or Negro, Indian (Amer.) (Print the name of the enrolled or principal tribe.), Eskimo, Aleut, and Other race (Print race). There was also a seventh race, Asian or Pacific Islander (API), which required one to choose one of ten sub-categories: Japanese, Chinese, Filipino, Korean, Vietnamese, Asian Indian, Hawaiian, Guamanian, Samoan, Other API. There was also a separate question, "Is this person of Spanish/Hispanic origin or descent?" with substantially the same five options as in the 1980 census.

The 2000 census made a few changes from that of 1990—most notably allowing individuals to choose one or more races. It changed "Race" to "What is this person's race?" It dropped the Asian or Pacific Islander (API) race category, and simply merged all its subcategories with the other races; and it changed "Guamanian" to "Guamanian or Chamorro." The 2010 census race question was substantially the same as that of 2000, yielding the current fifteen races: (1) White; (2) Black, African American, or Negro; (3) American Indian or Alaskan Native (and leaves a space for you to write in your enrolled or principal tribe); (4) Asian Indian; (5) Chinese; (6) Filipino; (7) Japanese; (8) Korean; (9) Vietnamese; (10) Other Asian (and leaves a space for you to write in your race); (11) Native Hawaiian; (12) Guamanian or Chamorro; (13) Samoan; (14) Other Pacific Islander (and leaves a space for you to write in your race); and (15) Some other race (and leaves a space for you to write in your race).

Even though it has insisted on reifying the term "race" ever since 1990, the census has kept changing the names of races, the ways races are categorized, and the number of races.

Name changes: Guamanian became Guamanian or Chamorro; Black or Negro became Black, African American, or Negro.

Category changes: Asian or Pacific Islander was a race with subcategories in 1990; but in 2000 and 2010 it became eleven races. (One might also ask why Guamanian and Samoan are considered separate races, but Other Pacific Islander merges numerous possibilities—such as Tahitian—into a single race. Is U. S. citizenship the distinguishing feature of a race—Tahitians are French—and if so, how can race be a biological category?)

Changes in the number of races: Seven races in 1990 became fifteen in 2000 and 2010.

If there is one conclusion that is clear from the three most recent censuses—as has been evident in the discussion in the previous sections—it is that racial categories are actually political and cultural categories created in response to social pressures, and not biological entities.

What Have We Learned?

Looking over the "race" questions on the twenty-three censuses from 1790 through 2010—variously labeled as (a) free white/other free/slave, (b) color, (c) color or race, (d) is this person, and (e) race—and the widely varied options for answering them, it is easy to see that they have varied greatly over time.

Several trends are evident in these variations. These include: (1) a shift from "slave versus free" as a classifier to "race"; (2) the separation of race from Latin American descent; (3) oscillation between allowing for self-description ("is this person") and insistence on a race label; (4) oscillation between allowing for multiple descriptors and insisting on a

single descriptor; and (5) proliferation of categories over a series of censuses followed by regrouping with a smaller number of options. If asked to fill out all twenty-three forms,
many individuals in our increasingly diverse country would
have to change the way they label themselves multiple times.

Those responsible for preparing the 2010 census would
probably argue for the desirability of continuing the 2000
practice of using the category "race" along with substantially
the same options. They would say that this allows for compa-
rability of data so that population trends can be more accurately monitored. There are several responses to this argument.

To begin with, the census has been notably inconsistent in
its terminology over the decades, so that to aim for consistency
with the use of the scientifically untenable "race" category is to
knowingly propagate error. In the words of Oscar Wilde,
"Consistency is the last refuge of the unimaginative." Or, in
computer speak, GIGO (garbage in/garbage out).

Since race is a socially constructed category rather than a
scientifically observable one, and because social concepts vary
as the culture changes, the assumption that the same term
maintains the same meaning over time is inaccurate. For example, while individuals continue to list the identical date of
birth every ten years, they may change their racial self-desig-
nation over the same period of time, even when choosing
from an identical list of options. One instance of this is the
increase in the number of "American Indians" following the
introduction of casinos on reservations.

The statement on the U. S. government website that the
race question has been "Asked since 1790" is inaccurate and
misleading. The statement is inaccurate because the term
"race" didn't appear until 1900, and it is misleading because it
implies that the same question has been asked on all twenty-

three censuses. As this chapter has shown in great detail, the questions, the categories within the questions, and the options within the categories have varied wildly over time, with no element in common over the 220-year time span. By using cultural terms masquerading as biological ones, the use of the term "race" has had the effect of legitimizing an unscientific and (to many) offensive question.

Let us hope that the 2020 census will acknowledge science and abandon the term "race"—perhaps by reintroducing some form of the "Is this person" question.

Barack Obama's Twenty-Three Races

In filling out his 2010 census form, President Obama chose a single option for his race from the fifteen offered: "Black, African Am., or Negro." As we have seen, slavery, the Civil War, segregation, immigration, civil rights legislation, and intermarriage are some of the main contributors to Americans' changing cultural conceptions of race, and to the changing categories in the census. As a result, people in the United States may change their race over time. While they look the same, and have the same genes and ancestry, they may change the ways they categorize themselves, others may change the ways they label them, and the census may change the ways it classifies them.

Obama's race—like that of numerous other Americans—would also have changed over time. While individuals with even more complex backgrounds than his (e.g., four grandparents from four different parts of the world) would produce even more varied responses to the census questions, our president clearly personifies these changes.

This is how Obama might today answer the relevant questions on all twenty-three censuses:

1790–1810	Other free person
1820	Either "other free person except Indians" or "colored person"
1830–1840	Free black male over 36 and under 55
1850–1860	Free inhabitant/color—mulatto
1870–1880	Color—mulatto (M)
1890	Mulatto
1900–1940	Personal description/color or race (left to the individual to answer)—Black
1950	Race—Negro (Neg)
1960	Is this person—Negro
1970	Color or race—Negro or Black
1980	Is this person—Black or Negro
1990	Race—Black or Negro
2000–2010	What is this person's race?—Black, African Am., or Negro

People with more complex backgrounds—for example, with four grandparents of African, British, Chinese, and Mexican descent—would have confronted more varied and difficult choices. And the president's sister, Maya Soetoro-Ng, might often have been among the many individuals listed as "other" because the censuses have never had a category for Indonesian ancestry.

Clearly the options available for individuals to label themselves have varied greatly over time. Even more significantly, however, the categories to which the options belong have themselves changed: from (a) free white/other free/slave, to (b) color, to (c) color or race, to (d) is this person, to (e) race.

The multiple changes in ways our president would have classified himself over the twenty-three censuses make it obvious that race is an American cultural concept that has varied over time and that can be expected to change in the future. For this reason, it would be desirable for future censuses to drop the unscientific biological-sounding classifier "race."

Lessons About Race from the Brazilian Census

As we have seen, race is a cultural concept, and beliefs about race vary dramatically from one culture to another. In this regard, America and Brazil are amazingly different in the categories they use. The United States has a small number of racial categories, based overwhelmingly on ancestry. Thus, it is possible for an American who "looks white" to "really be black" because he or she has "black blood."

In contrast, Brazilians classify people according to what they look like, using a large number of different terms. For example, one study in the Brazilian northeast conducted by the *Instituto Brasileiro de Geografia e Estatística* (IBGE)—the entity responsible for the census—asked people what color (*cor*) they were, and received 134 different answers. (Other studies have found even larger numbers, and the results vary regionally, with much fewer categories used in the south of the country.) In many Brazilian families different racial terms are used to refer to different children, while such distinctions are not possible in the United States because all the children—no matter what they look like—have the same ancestry.

Thus, I was fascinated to read, "For the first time, non-white people make up the majority of Brazil's population, according to preliminary results of the 2010 census."

Slavery was much more widespread in Brazil than in the United States (and ended only in 1888), with the number of Africans always outnumbering the number of Portuguese, and with Portuguese men probably fathering more offspring with African slaves than with Portuguese women. In fact, there is a saying in Brazil that everyone has "one foot in the kitchen"—meaning an ancestor who was an African slave. Thus, if Brazilians thought about race the way Americans do, it would always have been true that "non-white people make up the majority of Brazil's population." To put it more strongly, using American racial categories, Brazil has always had a majority black population.

Of course, Brazilians do not use American racial categories, and are critical of Americans for "calling people black who are not black." Put differently, Brazilians would say that the American census over-counts the number of blacks, while Americans would say that the Brazilian census over-counts the number of whites. Specifically, the 2010 Brazilian census lists 47.7 percent of the population as white, and only 7.6 percent as black—numbers that would seem unreal to visitors from the United States. (And 43.1 percent were classified as mixed.)

Just as American census categories of race are unscientific and do not correspond to the cultural categories Americans use to think about race, Brazilian census categories of race are also unscientific and also do not correspond to the cultural categories Brazilians use to think about race. For example, the largest number of non-white Brazilians would be classified as *pardo*, a census term that Americans can think of as roughly meaning *mixed*. However, *pardo* is a term that is rarely used in everyday speech. So the census categorizes tens of millions of Brazilians by a term they would not use to describe themselves or others.

The biological sciences tell us that the human species has no biological races—all that exists is gradual variation, with more distant populations differing more from one another than closer ones. The social sciences tell us that different cultures use different concepts of race to categorize people. And governments tell us what "racial" categories to use to count people.

CHAPTER 5

Racial Myths and
the Author's Family

Beginning with a puzzling example from my family, this chapter reviews some earlier material and considers additional biological and cultural specifics. Solving the puzzle leads to a more general discussion of the concept of race—in different cultures, as applied to children of intermarriage, and as confronted by immigrants.

A Racial Puzzle

After finishing college, my daughter lived for one year in Rio de Janeiro. During that time she returned home for a visit accompanied by her Brazilian boyfriend. I invited them to come to my cross-cultural psychology class to be interviewed about Brazilian culture, and they agreed. At one point in the interview I asked her, "Are you black?" She said, "Yes." I then asked him the question, and he said, "No."

"How can that be?" I asked the class. "He's darker than she is."

Puzzles like this remind us that discussions of race often confuse cultural classifications with biological ones. To solve the puzzle we need to divide the question "What is race?" into two more limited ones. And, as we have seen, both answers differ strikingly from what Americans think of as race.

The first question is, "How can we understand the variation in physical appearance among human beings?" It is interesting to discover that Americans view only a part of the variation as "racial," while other equally evident variability is not so viewed.

The second question is, "How can we understand the kinds of racial classifications applied to differences in physical appearance among human beings?" As has already been pointed out, different cultures label these physical differences in different ways. Far from describing biological entities, the American system of racial categories is merely one of numerous culture-specific schemes for reducing uncertainty about how people should respond to other people. The fact that Americans believe Asians, blacks, Latinos, and whites constitute biological entities called races is a matter of cultural interest rather than scientific substance. It tells us something about American culture, but it tells us nothing about the human species.

Why Do People Look Different?

To answer this first question, let's start by reviewing human physical variation. Human beings are a species, *Homo sapiens*, which means that people from anywhere on the planet can mate with others from anywhere else and produce fertile offspring.

Our species evolved in Africa from earlier forms and eventually spread out around the planet. Over time, human populations that were geographically separated from one another came to differ in physical appearance through three major pathways: mutation, natural selection, and genetic drift. Since genetic mutations occur randomly, different mutations occur and accumulate over time in geographically separated populations. Also, as we have known since the time of Charles Darwin, different geographical environments select for different physical traits that confer a survival advantage. But the largest proportion of variability among populations may well result from purely random factors; this random change in the frequencies of already existing genes is known as *genetic drift*.

If an earthquake or disease kills off a large segment of a population, those who survive to reproduce are likely to differ from the original population in many ways. Similarly, if a group divides and a subgroup moves away, the two groups will, by chance, differ in the frequency of various genes. Even the mere fact of physical separation will, over time, lead two equivalent populations to differ in the frequency of genes. These randomly acquired population differences, along with any others, will accumulate over successive generations due to mutation or natural selection.

A number of the differences in physical appearance among populations around the globe appear to have adaptive value. For example, people in the tropics of Africa and South America came to have dark skin, presumably, through natural selection, as protection against the sun. In cold areas, like northern Europe or northern North America, which can be without sunlight for long periods of time and where people covered their bodies for warmth, people came to have light skin—light skin makes maximum use of sunlight to produce vitamin D.

The indigenous peoples of the New World arrived about fifteen thousand years ago, during the last ice age, probably following wild game across the Bering Strait. (The sea level was low enough to create a land bridge because so much water was in the form of ice.) Thus, the dark-skinned Indians of the South American tropics are descended from lighter-skinned ancestors, similar in appearance to the Inuit. In other words, even though skin color is the most salient feature thought by Americans to be an indicator of race—and race is assumed to have great time depth—it is subject to relatively rapid evolutionary change.

Meanwhile, the extra ("epicanthic") fold of eyelid skin, which Americans also view as racial, and which evolved in Asian populations to protect the eye against the cold, continues to exist among South American native peoples because its presence (unlike a light skin) offers no reproductive disadvantage. Hence, skin color and eyelid form, which Americans think of as traits of different races, occur together or separately in different populations.

Like skin color, there are other physical differences that also appear to have evolved through natural selection—but which Americans do not think of as racial. Take, for example, body shape. Some populations in very cold climates, such as the Inuit, developed rounded bodies. This is because the more spherical an object is, the less surface area it has to radiate heat. In contrast, some populations in very hot climates, such as the Masai, developed lanky bodies. Like the tubular pipes of an old-fashioned radiator, the high ratio of surface area to volume allows people to radiate a lot of heat.

In terms of Americans' way of thinking about race, lanky people and rounded people are simply two kinds of whites or blacks. But it is equally reasonable to view light-skinned people and dark-skinned people as two kinds of "lankys" or "roundeds." In other words, our categories for the racial classification of people arbitrarily include certain dimensions (light versus dark skin) and exclude others (rounded versus elongated bodies).

There is no biological basis for classifying race according to skin color instead of body form—or according to any other variable, for that matter. All that exists is variability in what people look like and the arbitrary and culturally specific ways different societies classify that variability. There is nothing left over that can be called race. This is why biological race is a myth.

Skin color and body form do not vary together: Not all dark-skinned people are lanky; similarly, light-skinned people may be lanky or rounded. The same can be said of the facial features Americans think of as racial—eye color, nose width (actually, the ratio of width to length), lip thickness ("evertedness"), hair form, and hair color. They do not vary together either. If they did, then a "totally white" person would have very light skin color, straight blond hair, blue eyes, a narrow nose, and thin lips; a "totally black" person would have very dark skin color, black tight-curly hair, dark brown eyes, a broad nose, and thick lips; those in between would have—to a correlated degree—light wavy brown hair, light brown eyes, and intermediate nose and lip forms.

While people of mixed European and African ancestry who look like this do exist, they are the exception rather than the rule. As indicated previously, anyone who wants to can make up a chart of facial features (choose a location with a diverse population, say, the New York City subway) and verify that there are people with all possible admixtures of facial features. One might see someone with tight-curly, blond hair, light skin, blue eyes, broad nose, and thick lips—whose features are half black and half white. That is, each of the person's facial features occupies one end or the other of a supposedly racial continuum, with no intermediary forms (like light, wavy brown hair). Such people are living proof that supposedly racial features do not vary together.

Since the human species has spent most of its existence in Africa, different populations in Africa have been separated from each other longer than East Asians or Northern Europeans have been separated from each other or from sub-Saharan Africans. As a result, there is remarkable physical variation among the peoples of Africa, which goes unrecognized by Americans who view them all as belonging to the same race.

In contrast to the very tall Masai, the diminutive stature of the very short Pygmies may have evolved as an advantage in moving rapidly through tangled forest vegetation. The Bushmen of the Kalahari Desert have very large ("steatopygous") buttocks, presumably to store body fat in one place for times of food scarcity, while leaving the rest of the body less insulated to radiate heat. They also have "peppercorn" hair. Hair in separated tufts, like tight-curly hair, leaves space to radiate the heat that rises through the body to the scalp; straight hair lies flat and holds in body heat, like a cap. By viewing Africans as constituting a single race, Americans ignore their greater physical variability, while assigning racial significance to lesser differences between them.

Although it is true that most inhabitants of northern Europe, east Asia, and sub-Saharan Africa look like Americans' conceptions of one or another of the three purported races, most inhabitants of south Asia, southwest Asia, north Africa, and the Pacific islands do not. Thus, the eighteenth-century view of the human species as comprised of Caucasoid, Mongoloid, and Negroid races, still held by many Americans, is based on a partial and unrepresentative view of human variability. In other words, what is now known about human physical variation does not correspond to what Americans think of as race.

How Do Cultures Categorize Differences in Appearance?

In contrast to the question of the actual physical variation among human beings, there is the question of how people classify that variation. Scientists classify things in scientific taxonomies—for example, chemists' periodic table of the elements, or biologists' classification of life forms into kingdoms, phyla, and so forth.

In every culture, people also classify things along culture-specific dimensions of meaning. For example, paper clips and staples are understood by Americans as paper fasteners, and nails are not, even though, in terms of their physical properties, all three consist of differently shaped pieces of metal wire. The physical variation in pieces of metal wire can be seen as analogous to human physical variation; and the categories of cultural meaning, like paper fasteners versus wood fasteners, can be seen as analogous to races. Anthropologists refer to these kinds of classifications as folk taxonomies.

Reviewing Avocados and Folk Taxonomies

Remember the question about the avocado: Is it a fruit or a vegetable? Americans insist it is a vegetable. We eat it in salads with oil and vinegar. Brazilians, on the other hand, would say it is a fruit. They eat it for dessert with lemon juice and sugar.

How can we explain this difference in classification?

The avocado is an edible plant, and the American and Brazilian folk taxonomies, while containing cognate terms, classify some edible plants differently. The avocado does not change. It is the same biological entity; but its folk classification changes, depending on who's doing the classifying.

Human beings are also biological entities. Just as we can ask if an avocado is a fruit or a vegetable, we can ask if a person is white or black. And when we ask race questions, the answers we get come from folk taxonomies, not scientific ones. Terms like "white" or "black" applied to people—or "vegetable" or "fruit" applied to avocados—do not give us biological information about people or avocados. Rather, they exemplify how cultural groups (Brazilians or Americans) classify people and avocados.

More on Americans and "Blood"

As was discussed earlier, Americans believe in "blood," a folk term for the quality presumed to be carried by members of so-called races. And the way offspring—regardless of their physical appearance—always inherit the less prestigious racial category of mixed parentage is called "hypo-descent" by anthropologists. A sentence thoroughly intelligible to most Americans might be, "Since Mary's father is white, and her mother is black, Mary is black because she has black 'blood.'" American researchers who think they are studying racial differences in behavior would, like other Americans, classify Mary as black—although she has just as much white "blood."

According to hypo-descent, the various purported racial categories are arranged in a hierarchy along a single dimen-

sion, from the most prestigious ("white"), through intermediary forms ("Asian"), to the least prestigious ("black"). And
when a couple comes from two different categories, all
their children (the "descent" in "hypo-descent") are classified as belonging to the less prestigious category (thus, the
"hypo"). Hence, all the offspring of one "white" parent and
one "black" parent—regardless of the children's physical appearance—have traditionally been called "black" in the
United States.

The American folk concept of "blood" does not behave like
genes. Genes are units that cannot be subdivided. When several
genes jointly determine a trait, chance decides which ones come
from each parent. As indicated previously, if eight genes determine a trait, a child gets four from each parent. If a mother and
a father each have the hypothetical genes BBBBWWWW,
then a child could be born with any combination of B and W
genes, from BBBBBBBB to WWWWWWWW. In con-
trast, the folk concept "blood" behaves like a uniform and
continuous entity. It can be divided in two repeatedly—for
example, quadroons and octoroons are said to be people who
have one-quarter and one-eighth black "blood," respectively.
As indicated in the last chapter, the 1890 census actually
counted Americans in these categories.

Oddly, because of hypo-descent, Americans consider people
with one-eighth black "blood" to be black rather than white, despite their having seven-eighths white "blood." Furthermore,
the 1890 census categories leave out many people from their intended arithmetic precision. For example, the offspring of a
black and a mulatto would have six-eighths black blood; the offspring of that person and a black would have seven-eighths
black blood; the offspring of a black and a quadroon would have
five-eighths black blood; and the offspring of a mulatto and a

quadroon would have three-eighths black blood. No terms exist for any of these people—illustrating that the proliferation of racial categories only creates more places for individuals to fall through the cracks.

Hypo-descent, or "blood," is not informative about the physical appearance of people. For example, when two parents called black in the United States have a number of children, the children are likely to vary in physical appearance. In the case of skin color, they might vary from lighter than the lighter parent to darker than the darker parent. Traditionally, however, they have all received the same racial classification—black—regardless of their skin color.

All that hypo-descent tells you is that, when someone is classified as something other than white (e.g., Asian), at least one of his or her parents is classified in the same way, and that neither parent has a less prestigious classification (e.g., black). That is, hypo-descent is informative about ancestry—specifically, parental classification—rather than physical appearance.

There are many strange consequences of our folk taxonomy. For example, a white woman can give birth to a black baby (e.g., President Obama) but a black woman cannot give birth to a white baby because the baby would have the mother's black "blood." Such an offspring, who inherited no genes that produce "African"-appearing physical features, would traditionally still be considered black because he or she has a parent classified as black. The category "passing for white" includes many such people. Americans have the curious belief that people who look white but have a parent classified as black are "really" black in some biological sense, and are being deceptive if they present themselves as white. Such examples make it clear that race is a social rather than a physical classification.

How Cultural Beliefs About Race
Affect Visual Perception

From infancy, human beings learn to recognize very subtle differences in the faces of those around them. Black babies see a wider variety of black faces than white faces, and white babies see a wider variety of white faces than black faces. Because they are exposed to only a limited range of human variation, adult members of each "race" come to see their own group as containing much wider variation than others. Thus, because of this perceptual learning, blacks see greater physical variation among themselves than among whites, while whites see the opposite. In this case, however, there is a clear answer to the question of which group contains greater physical variability. Blacks are correct.

Why is this the case?

It is often difficult to persuade white people to accept what at first appears to contradict the evidence they can see clearly with their own eyes—but which is really the result of a history of perceptual learning. However, the reason that blacks view themselves as more varied is not that their vision is more accurate. Rather, it is that blacks too have a long—but different—history of perceptual learning from that of whites (and also that they have been observers of a larger range of human variation).

The fact of greater physical variation among blacks than whites in America goes back to the principle of hypo-descent, which classifies all people with one black parent and one white parent as black. If they were all considered white, then there would be more physical variation among whites. Someone with one-eighth white "blood" and seven-eighths black "blood" would be considered white; anyone with any white ancestry would be considered white. In other words, what appears to be a difference in biological variability is really a perceptual phenomenon stemming from a difference in cultural classification.

American Races and Brazilian *Tipos*

Perhaps the clearest way to understand that the American folk taxonomy of race is merely one of many—arbitrary and unscientific like all the others—is to contrast it with a very different one, that of Brazil. The Portuguese word that in the Brazilian folk taxonomy corresponds to the American *race* is *tipo* (though Brazilians sometimes use the word *cor* [color] in the same way). *Tipo*, a cognate of the English word *type*, is a descriptive term that serves as a kind of shorthand for a series of physical features. Because people's physical features vary separately from one another, there are an awful lot of *tipos* in Brazil.

Since *tipos* are descriptive terms, they vary regionally in Brazil—in part because they are most elaborated in the Northeast, which was the historical epicenter of slavery, in part reflecting regional differences in the development of colloquial Portuguese, and in part because the physical variation they describe is different in different regions. The Brazilian situation is so complex, I will limit my delineation of *tipos* to some of the main ones used in the city of Salvador, Bahia, to describe people whose physical appearance is understood to be made up of African and European features. (I will use the female terms throughout; in nearly all cases the male term simply changes the last letter from "a" to "o.")

Proceeding along a dimension from the "whitest" to the "blackest" *tipos*, a *loura* is whiter-than-white, with straight, blond hair, blue or green eyes, light skin color, narrow nose, and thin lips. Brazilians who come to the United States think that a *loura* is a *blond*, and are surprised to find that the American term refers to hair color only. A *branca* has light skin color, eyes of any color, hair of any color or form except tight curly, a nose that is not broad, and lips that are not thick. *Branca* translates as "white," though Brazilians of this *tipo* who come to the United States—especially those from elite families—are often dismayed to find that they are not considered white here and, even worse, are viewed as Hispanic despite the fact that they speak Portuguese.

A *morena* has brown or black hair that is wavy or curly but not tight curly, tan skin, a nose that is not narrow, and lips that are not thin. Brazilians who come to the United States think that a *morena* is a *brunette* and are surprised to find that brunettes are considered white but *morenas* are not. Americans have difficulty classifying *morenas*, many of whom are of Latin American origin: Are they black or Hispanic? (One might also observe that *morenas* have trouble with Americans, for not just accepting their appearance as a given, but asking instead, "Where do you come from?" "What language did you speak at home?" "What was your maiden name?" or even, more crudely, "What are you?")

A *mulata* looks like a *morena*, except with tight-curly hair and a slightly darker range of hair colors and skin colors. A *preta* looks like a *mulata*, except with dark brown skin, broad nose, and thick lips. To Americans, *mulatas* and *pretas* are both black and if forced to distinguish between them would refer to them as light-skinned blacks and dark-skinned blacks, respectively.

If Brazilians were forced to divide the range of *tipos*, from *loura* to *preta*, into "kinds of whites" and "kinds of blacks" (a distinction they do not ordinarily make), they would draw the line between *morenas* and *mulatas*; whereas Americans, if offered only visual information, would draw the line between *brancas* and *morenas*.

The proliferation of *tipos*, and the difference in the white-black dividing line, does not, however, exhaust the differences between Brazilian and American folk taxonomies. There are *tipos* in the Afro-European domain that are considered to be neither black nor white—an idea that is difficult for Americans visiting Brazil to comprehend. A person with tight-curly, blond (or red) hair, light skin, blue (or green) eyes, broad nose, and thick lips, is a *sarará*. The opposite features—straight, black hair, dark skin, brown eyes, narrow nose, and thin lips—are those of a *cabo verde*. *Sarará* and *cabo verde* are both *tipos* that are considered by Brazilians in Salvador, Bahia, to be neither black nor white.

How My Daughter Changed Her Race

When I interviewed my American daughter and her Brazilian boyfriend, she said she was black because her mother is black (even though I am white). That is, from her American perspective, she has "black blood"—though she is a *morena* in Brazil. Her boyfriend said that he was not black because, in terms of Brazilian tipos, he is a *mulato* (not a *preto*).

There are many differences between the Brazilian and American folk taxonomies of race. The American system tells you about how people's parents are classified but not what they look like. The Brazilian system tells you what they look like but not about their parents. When two parents of intermediate appearance have many children in the United States, the children are all of one race; in Brazil they are of many *tipos*.

Americans believe that race is an immutable biological given, but people (like my daughter and her boyfriend) can change their race by getting on a plane and going from the United States to Brazil—just as, if they take an avocado with them, it changes from a vegetable into a fruit. In both cases, what changes is not the physical appearance of the person or avocado (nor for that matter their genes or ancestry) but the way they are classified.

I have focused on the Brazilian system to make clear how profoundly folk taxonomies of race vary from one place to another. But the Brazilian system is just one of many. Haiti's folk taxonomy, for example, includes elements of both ancestry and physical appearance, and even includes the amazing term (for foreigners of African appearance) *un blanc noir*—literally, "a black white."

In his classic 1964 study, *Patterns of Race in the Americas*, the anthropologist Marvin Harris introduced readers to the ways in which the conquests by differing European powers of differing New World peoples and ecologies combined with differing patterns of slavery to produce a variety of folk taxonomies. So the fact that categories of race vary from one culture to another has been well known for about a half-century.

Folk taxonomies of race can be found in many—though by no means all—cultures in other parts of the world as well; and the last chapter discusses the spread of the race concept.

American Races and Indian Castes

In many ways, American beliefs about race are similar to Indian beliefs about caste. The United States and India both have cultural practices aimed at maintaining social distance between people from different categories; and these practices affect where they live, what work they do, whom they work with, and whom they associate with.

Americans believe you are born into a race that you cannot change and discourage marriages between races. Indians believe that you are born into a caste that you cannot change, and discourage marriages between castes. For many Americans, interracial marriages that are discouraged in the United States would not be discouraged in Brazil because Brazilians do not share our system of racial categories. And for many Indians, intercaste marriages that are discouraged in India would not be discouraged in the United States because Americans do not share the Indian system of caste categories.

When Immigrants Confront the American Idea of Race

Immigrants of varied physical appearance come to the United States from countries with racial folk taxonomies different from our own (not to mention other folk taxonomies, including caste, ethnicity, and religion). They are often perplexed and dismayed to find that the ways they classify themselves and others are irrelevant to the American reality. Brazilians, Haitians, and others may find themselves labeled by strange, apparently inappropriate, and even pejorative terms, and grouped together with people who are different from and unreceptive to them. This can cause psychological complications. For example, imagine a Brazilian immigrant who views himself as white being treated by an American therapist who assumes that he is not.

Immigration has increased, especially from geographical regions whose people do not resemble American images of blacks, whites, or Asians. Intermarriage is also increasing, as the stigma associated with it diminishes. These two trends are augmenting the physical diversity among those who marry each other—and, as a result, among their children. The American folk taxonomy of race (purportedly comprised of stable biological entities) is beginning to change to accommodate this new reality. After all, what race are people whose four grandparents are black, white, Asian, and Latino? Traditionally, they would be called *black*, but today many Americans would consider them *mixed*. And the single term *mixed* is hardly adequate to denote the varieties of physical appearance and ancestry to which it is applied.

Thinking in terms of physical appearance and folk taxonomies helps to clarify the emotionally charged but confused topic of race. Understanding that different cultures have different folk taxonomies suggests that we respond to the question "What race is that person?" not by "Black," or "White," but by "Where?" and "When?"

CHAPTER 6

Myths about Race and Intelligence

Since the human species has no races in the biological sense, and since conceptions of race vary widely from one culture to another, assertions of biologically based racial differences in intelligence are scientifically meaningless. An understanding of key IQ-relevant issues—like heritability, twin studies, different kinds of minorities, and the role of formal education—leads to social and cultural explanations for group differences. It also leads to suggestions for ways parents can raise smarter kids.

What Do IQ Tests Measure?

Since discussions of intelligence begin with IQ tests, let's start by considering the reason we need tests in the first place. Tests offer a shorthand way of measuring something complicated or extensive. Here is a simplified illustration—a multiplication test might use a sample of ten questions to determine whether children have learned all one hundred cells in the times table. One question might be "7 x 7 = ?" but the question "7 x 8 = ?" might not be asked.

Consider two students who might have learned most but not all of the 7 table. One might know 7 x 7 but not 7 x 8, and the opposite might be true for the other. Thus, despite equivalent knowledge, the one who knew 7 x 7 would score higher on the test. Similarly, a student who didn't get much sleep the previous night or whose parents were going through a divorce might have more trouble concentrating and do more poorly than a well-rested one with equivalent knowledge living in a happy home. Despite these limitations, in general, students who learned more of the times table would get higher scores.

In other words, tests provide useful information, but they vary in how well they accomplish their task; and all are imperfect measures to a greater or lesser degree.

Many people believe that IQ tests measure intellectual potential; but when you think about it, it is easy to see that that cannot be the case. Whether attempting to measure how well students have learned the times table, or a more abstract cognitive process such as how well they understand the concept of multiplication, tests record participants' performance and use that as an estimate of the more general concern. For example, the ten-item multiplication test estimates how well students have learned all one hundred items of the multiplication table. Since, however, potential is not a quality that can be observed, it is not something that can be measured.

Early attempts to measure intelligence were aimed at testing the efficiency of the nervous system by measuring abilities such as reaction time—and these failed miserably. In contrast, the first successful IQ tests, early in the twentieth century, were aimed at identifying mentally retarded children—and these tests consisted of tasks similar to those that children might encounter in school. In other words, rather than measuring potential, the tests measure the kinds of intellectual behavior that lead to school success.

Children with high IQs and low grades have been referred to as *underachievers*, and—even more absurdly—those with low IQs and high grades have been called *overachievers*. It is as if school performance—the target measure—has somehow become secondary, while the test score has magically become the primary concern. By definition, one's potential sets an upper limit on performance, so that the idea of achieving more than one's potential is a contradiction in terms. The obvious explanation is that IQ tests are imperfect measures, so it is to be expected that some students will do better or worse in school than their scores would suggest.

There are various forms of intelligence not measured by IQ tests, from street smarts to musical ability. IQ tests measure the kinds of academic abilities and knowledge that contribute to school success, and—as is discussed below—that are increased by formal education.

The Problem With Twin Studies

Psychologists use IQ tests to measure intelligence, and they attempt to separate the effects of genes and environment on intelligence by examining whether more closely related individuals have more closely related IQs. Since identical twins are the most closely related pairs one can find in nature, a key source of evidence is provided by twin studies.

Identical twins are formed from a single ovum fertilized by a single sperm; at some early point the zygote divides and

gives rise to two separate fetuses. Identical twins share all
their genes and, therefore, are always of the same sex.

Fraternal twins are formed from two different ova fertilized by two different sperm. Essentially, fraternal twins are
siblings born at the same time. Like other siblings they
share half their genes, and half the time they are of different
sexes.

In its simplest form, the logic behind twin studies argues
that, since twins are the same age and are raised together in
the same family, their environments are substantially the
same. Therefore, if identical twins are more similar in some
behavior than fraternal twins, the genes they share must cause
the increased similarity.

There are problems with the assumption that twins raised
in the same family share substantially the same environment,
but that is not what this section is about. It is about the prenatal environment.

The prenatal environment is arguably the most important
environment in an individual's life. Environmental effects on
the developing fetus can lead to a wide variety of subtle and
profound lifelong alterations. The mother's health and nutri-
tion, illnesses and accidents, level of stress, exposure to environmental toxins, medications, and alcohol, cigarettes, and
other psychoactive substances are among the numerous environmental influences on the developing fetus.

Twin studies make the unjustified assumption that twins
share the same prenatal environment. Actually, fraternal twins
develop two placentas that can fuse together and appear to be
one, while most identical twins share the same placenta. Clearly,
two fetuses supported by the same placenta share a more similar
environment than two fetuses supported by two different placentas. In addition, different genes interacting with the same envi-

ronment often produce different results. Thus, identical twins' genes may produce identical prenatal gene-environment interactions, while fraternal twins' genes may produce differing prenatal gene-environment interactions.

In a similar way, fraternal twins share a more similar prenatal environment than do siblings; and fraternal twins are more similar to each other in IQ (and rates of schizophrenia) than are siblings.

In other words, identical twins in utero have identical genes and more similar prenatal environments and more similar prenatal gene-environment interactions. Thus, one cannot conclude that if identical twins are more similar in IQ (or some other behavior) than fraternal twins, the increased similarity must be caused by the genes they share. Instead, the conclusion should be that the greater similarity results from both the genes that identical twins share and their more similar prenatal environments. Put another way, twin studies fail to separate the effects of genes and the prenatal environment. This failure casts doubt on claims of the relative effects of genes and environment on intelligence, psychiatric disorders, personality and other psychological variables, and other conditions.

One way to separate the effects of genes and prenatal environment would be to do a study that compares identical twins who shared one placenta with identical twins from two placentas.

Why Heritability Does Not Mean Genetic Causation

In discussing IQ tests and twin studies, researchers often make use of the heritability statistic. Heritability is expressed as a number that varies from 0 to 1, or from 0 percent to 100 percent. Although the term sounds as if it has to do with inheritance, people are sometimes surprised to learn that it is not derived from observations of genes or chromosomes.

Individuals have genes that cause them, for example, to have five fingers on each hand. When there aren't five fingers, the cause is almost always environmental (e.g., prenatal thalidomide, or a post-natal accident). In contrast, the heritability statistic applies to populations—not individuals. Technically speaking, heritability is the percentage of genetically associated variation in a population under given environmental conditions. Another way of saying this is that it is the ratio of genetically associated variation to all variation (both environmentally and genetically associated).

There are three key terms to pay attention to in the definition of heritability. The first is *associated*. That is, unlike genes causing fingers, high heritability need not imply causation. Second is *under given environmental conditions*. That is, under different environmental conditions the heritability statistic could be either higher or lower. The third is that *heritability* refers to differences in a population, not to individual specifics (e.g., "the heritability of third graders' IQs" but not "the heritability of Mary's IQ").

For example, in the 1950s over 95 percent of medical students were men, so medical school attendance was highly heritable. If you knew that someone was a medical student you could guess with a high degree of accuracy that that person had an XY chromosome (i.e., was male) and not an XX chromosome (female). In the 2010s, women make up nearly half of American medical students, so today medical school attendance is not very heritable. Since medical students have to be intelligent—"have high medical intelligence"—people in the 1950s might have argued fallaciously that the high heritability of medical school attendance showed that women lacked the kind of intelligence necessary for medical school success, or even that they lacked the genes for medical intelligence. They might even have hypothesized that genes for medical intelligence could be found on the Y chromosome.

Clearly, attending medical school is not genetic in the sense of having five fingers. And as the environment changed—as educational opportunities opened up for women and gender role expectations changed over the last sixty years—the heritability declined.

Another way of putting this would be to say that IQ, like medical school attendance, may be highly heritable under certain conditions but need not be genetically determined. Or one might say that heritability estimates are correlations (between genetic variation and observable [phenotypic] variation), and that one cannot infer causality from correlations. In contrast, genetic explanations are causal (e.g., XX chromosomes produce females and XY chromosomes produce males). Thus, the term "heritability" sounds as if it offers a causal genetic explanation, but it does not.

Why Twin Studies and the Heritability of IQ Do Not Have Much to Say About Race

Using twin studies of IQ test scores and heritability studies, the next step in the race-IQ discussion is often to compare the scores of blacks and whites (and sometimes of other purported races such as Asians, Jews, Latinos, and American Indians). However, the heritability of IQ *within* the socially constructed category of American blacks and/or *within* the socially constructed category of American whites says nothing about IQ differences *between* the groups. This is because heritability refers to the relative ranking of individuals within a distribution rather than their actual scores. Helpful environmental effects can raise the entire distribution, and harmful environmental effects can lower it.

Some people have made the following fallacious argument. Because whites on average have higher IQs than blacks on average, and because twin studies have shown that IQ is highly heritable, therefore whites' higher IQs result from genetic superiority.

The fallacy arises from not considering environmental differences. Let us imagine a group of black identical twins separated and adopted at birth in the United States, and a similar group of white identical twins. For every pair, both black twins would be treated as black, and both white twins would be treated as white—creating significant postnatal environmental differences between the black and white groups, even if each set of twins has identical genes.

Table 6.1 illustrates the same point, this time using the adoptive parents' socioeconomic and educational background instead of race:

TABLE 6.1 Hypothetical IQ Data of Identical Twins Reared Apart

Twin Pair	Stimulating/ Advantaged Background	Disadvantaged Background
A	115	100
B	110	95
C	105	90
IQ Average	110	95
IQ Difference	15	
Correlation between IQs of Twins	1.0 (100%)	

The table shows that very high IQ heritability can occur at the same time as large between-group differences. In all three pairs, twin A has the highest IQ, twin B is in the middle, and twin C has the lowest. However, the advantaged background produces substantially higher IQs than the disadvantaged background.

(The situation is a bit more complicated than the table indicates because people have varied interests and abilities—from mathematical, linguistic, naturalistic, and other academic ones to social-emotional, athletic, musical, artistic, practical, and other non-academic areas. Both formal education and other life experiences give individuals an opportunity to pursue their interests and strengths, thereby developing certain abilities, while letting others remain relatively fallow. As a result, in addition to environments shifting the entire distribution of IQ scores up or down, one would expect them to cause a certain amount of reshuffling over time within the distribution. For example, students who are good in math and English, who have good instruction, who like the subjects, and who spend extra time in relevant activities such as studying, practicing math, reading, writing, doing crossword puzzles, playing word games, and solving logical problems, would tend to have their IQs go up relative to others in the distribution who neglect those areas and focus more on sports and social activities.)

Here is another fallacious argument that attempts to reach a conclusion about the cause of between-group differences in IQ from knowledge of within-group heritability. (We can assume for the sake of this argument that the current heritability of IQ is 100 percent for both American whites and American blacks.) Since whites on average score higher than blacks on average, it is possible that all of the difference is genetic, or some of the difference is genetic, or none of the difference is genetic. The most reasonable guess is that neither extreme is correct, and that some of the difference is genetic, and some is environmental.

What is the flaw in the argument? It doesn't consider all the possibilities. Here is a better version. Given that American whites on average currently score higher than American blacks on average, and that there are prenatal and postnatal environmental differences between whites and blacks, what are the possible outcomes if all environmental effects could somehow be equalized? Whites might score higher, both groups might have the same average scores, or blacks might score higher.

Studies of "identical twins reared apart compared to those reared together" also illustrate the much more limited view of "environment" (i.e., the United States today) that psychologists have, as compared to that of anthropologists. The studies do not compare one of each pair of twins raised by American college professors with the other raised by Brazilian Indians. Hence, in anthropological terms, the American studies are of "identical twins reared in very similar environments compared to those reared in extremely similar environments." By restricting the range of "environments" to American environments, the heritability estimate increases correspondingly.*

---

*Here are some illustrative numbers to show how changing the range of environments can affect heritability. The heritability statistic is a fraction—the genetically associated variation in a population under given environmental conditions divided by all variation (both genetically and environmentally associated). For very similar environments, suppose the genetically associated variation is 0.09 and the environmentally associated variation is much smaller, say 0.01. Then the heritability is 0.09/0.09 + 0.01 = 0.09/0.10 = 0.9 or 90 percent. In contrast, for very varied environments, suppose that the genetically associated variation is still 0.09 but that the environmentally associated variation is much greater, say 0.81. In this case the heritability is 0.09/0.09 + 0.81 = 0.09/0.90 = 0.1 or 10 percent.

Interestingly, psychologists have known for several decades that IQs have been rising in countries around the globe—at least since before World War II, and possibly for as long as IQ has been measured. This phenomenon is known as the *Flynn Effect*, named for the New Zealand political scientist James R. Flynn who brought it to the world's attention. One psychologist estimated that the average IQ in the United States in 1932, if today's tests had been used, would have been 80, with a substantial part of the population falling in a range now considered to be mentally retarded.

How might we make sense of this finding? Clearly there was insufficient time for the Flynn Effect to be the result of natural selection for smartness genes; so environmental changes are the obvious candidate for an explanation. Increased urbanization, more and more widespread formal education, and increases in literacy and test-taking skills are reasonable contenders as causes. One way of combining the Flynn Effect with black-white IQ differences in the United States would be to view American blacks as living in an educational environment comparable to that for American whites a few decades ago. This is quite different from asserting that whites have better IQ genes.

As we have seen, studies of differences in behavior between American "populations" of "whites" and "blacks," which seek to find biological causes rather than social ones, make an ethnocentric assumption. They assume that blacks and whites are populations in some biological sense, as sub-units of the human species. (Most likely, the researchers make this assumption because they are American and understand race in terms of the American folk taxonomy.) In fact, though, researchers sort the groups by a social rule for statistical purposes. This can be demonstrated by asking researchers "How do you know that the white subjects are really white and the black subjects are really black?" There is no biological answer to this question because race as a biological category does not exist. All that researchers can do is say, "The tester classified them based on what they look like," or "Their school records listed their race," or otherwise give a social rather than a biological answer.

Here is a parallel example. Let us construct two "races,"— one of people with large hands (instead of light skin) and the other of people with small hands (instead of dark skin). While it is logically conceivable that subjects with large hands might do better on a test of visual memory (instead of IQ), it would be strange to conduct such a study, and even more misguided, if differences were found by some bizarre happenstance, to seek a genetic explanation for the "racial differences." For example, people might have larger hands because they are larger; they might be larger because they are healthier; and their better health might be responsible for their better visual memory.

Similarly, one might ask how black-white IQ differences in the United States compare with black-white IQ differences in Brazil. However, many people considered black in the United States would not be considered black in Brazil, and many people considered white in Brazil would not be considered white in the United States—so the question cannot even be tested scientifically. This is why, when American researchers study racial differences in behavior, in search of biological rather than social causes for differences between socially defined groups, they are wasting their time.

Naturally, everything said in this section about heritability and the IQs of blacks and whites applies equally to comparisons among men and women, or among other groups such as

Asians, Jews, Latinos, or American Indians, about whom biologically based IQ generalizations have been made.

Why Culture Has Something Important to Say About IQ

Now that we have examined the shortcomings of purported biological explanations for black-white IQ differences, we can turn to cultural explanations.

In science, answers to general questions are more useful than answers to specific ones, so it is important to come up with good general questions. The educational anthropologist John U. Ogbu considered the question "Why do blacks score lower than whites on IQ tests in the United States?" and found a useful cross-cultural way of broadening it. His version was, "As we look at IQ testing in different countries, why do some minority groups score lower than the majority group, while other minority groups do not? And when a group is represented in more than one country, are its IQ scores the same in different places?"

Ogbu made the key distinction between immigrant (voluntary) minorities, who move to a new country because they expect a better life, and non-immigrant (involuntary) minorities who were conquered and/or colonized by an occupying power, or were taken as slaves against their will. While voluntary minorities have many reasons to trust or at least cooperate pragmatically with the dominant culture and its schools and tests, involuntary minorities have many reasons to mistrust, doubt, actively or passively resist, or otherwise avoid cooperating with them.

As has already been discussed, in the United States (as well as in other countries) we convert minority status into folk biological categories of "race." For example, some have argued that Asian Americans score higher on IQ tests than whites and blacks, not because their cultures place a higher value on academic achievement, make a point of providing intellectual stimulation, and get children to study more, but because they have some kind of biological superiority in not-yet-discovered intelligence genes. However, the children of Hmong tribesmen who came to the United States following the war in Viet Nam have not done well in our schools despite being Asian, because their culture of origin did not emphasize academic achievement. In addition, American Indians who are involuntary minorities, score low on tests, but they are also descended from Asians. And Mexican Americans, who are classified as "Latino"—another lower-scoring "racial" category—have on average a greater percentage of New World ancestry than Native Americans and are therefore descended from Asians as well. However, they are not classified as "Indian" because that is a folk term that Americans only apply north of the border. In all cases, the labels applied to the groups are social constructions rather than biological categories, and the groups' performance is understandable socially (because they are minorities) but not "racially."

In the case of African Americans, Ogbu detailed the contributions of both American society and African Americans themselves to their lower IQ scores. The societal contributions include segregated and inferior education, job ceilings, intellectual denigration, and cultural and language biases. The contributions of African Americans include self-doubt stemming from the internalization of whites' belief that blacks are not intelligent, a folk theory of "making it" in which test scores and school credentials are not seen as important (because, historically, they were not perceived as helping blacks to succeed), an adaptation to an ecological niche where advanced cognitive skills were not necessary for the jobs available, and an ambivalent or oppositional group identity and cultural frame of reference. With regard to the last of these, Ogbu described peer pressure against getting good grades or high test scores or taking advanced classes or speaking standard American English—labeling it as "acting white."

Statistical claims—that the black-white test score gap may be narrowing but will never close because of race-based genetic differences—simply do not take into account what may appear to outsiders as a motivation on the part of many to do poorly. (Even if most blacks do not have this motivation, all that is necessary for it to affect black-white test score differences is for a greater proportion of blacks than whites to feel this way.)

One is reminded of the Gypsies, whose school-avoidance is legendary, who (accurately) view the schools as instruments for socializing their children into mainstream society, and who have chosen a survival strategy of group preservation through cultural isolation. As a unique nomadic culture that is everywhere a persecuted minority, Gypsies defy categorization, even as their oppositional behavior yields fascinating insights about both them and the larger societies within which they live. Not surprisingly, they cannot easily be classified as either a voluntary minority or an involuntary minority, since they have features of both.

For Gypsies, cultural isolation depends in a profound way on individuals voluntarily distancing themselves from the norms and aspirations of the larger society. As a result, a successful Gypsy is one who has avoided the stigma of extensive formal education, since such a person would not have had the opportunity to learn the intellectual and social skills essential to his or her own culture. When African American youth use low school achievement and low scores to maintain group solidarity and opt out of mainstream society, this can be seen as a similar strategy.

Gypsies can also be understood as following a strategy of provoking prejudice to confirm the need for group solidarity, thereby strengthening group boundaries. Social pressures among African American youth to limit school performance and test scores can be seen as functioning in a similar way, by confirming the intellectual prejudices of whites, and demonstrating the need for solidarity in response. We can see here yet one more mutually reinforcing way in which the American black-white cultural divide continues to perpetuate itself across the generations.

Of course, blacks in America are quite diverse culturally, and include immigrants from countries in the Caribbean, Africa, and elsewhere. These groups, like many other voluntary minorities, have done quite well academically—especially in comparison with African Americans who trace their roots back to slavery in this country. Immigrants may well ask themselves the question, "What are my life chances and that of my family in the United States, in comparison to what they would have been back home?" African Americans, on the other hand are more likely to ask, "What are my life chances and that of my family, in comparison to what they would have been if we were white?"

In addition to studying African Americans, Ogbu found evidence for a pattern of lower IQ scores among involuntary minorities around the world—in India, Europe, North America, New Zealand, and Japan. Of particular interest are his findings regarding two cultural groups, both of which are voluntary minorities in one society and involuntary minorities in another. The fact that they display poor intellectual performance as involuntary minorities but do well as voluntary minorities implies that it is the nature of the groups' minority social status—and not their biological inferiority—that explains their poor performance.

The Buraku outcasts in Japan, an involuntary minority who are physically indistinguishable from other Japanese, scored 16 points below the Ippan majority (comparable to the American black-white gap of 13 to 15 points); but in the United States where both groups are voluntary minorities, the Buraku score the same as or slightly higher than the Ippan. Koreans, who are an involuntary minority in Japan, do poorly in school there; but they do well in the United States and China where they are a voluntary minority.

In short, an understanding of the lower IQ test scores of African Americans and of other involuntary minorities around the world needs to take into account both their resistance to the majority culture (including its schools and tests) and the effects of the majority culture's unequal treatment of them.

How Cultural Assumptions About Intelligence Affect Child Rearing

Having examined cultural explanations for minority group performance on IQ tests, we can look cross-culturally at majority group views and practices. Different cultures view intelligence and formal schooling in different ways that lead them to differing strategies of child rearing. There are, of course, wide variations among parents within a given culture as well as among various Western and Eastern cultures. However, in order to contrast two ways of thinking, let us consider two oversimplified views that I will refer to as *American* and *Chinese*.

In the American version, individuals are seen as differing in innate abilities and talents, and there is a concern with providing the conditions to encourage these abilities to develop. The idea is to offer children experiences that will permit them to discover their unique interests and aptitudes and allow them to flourish. There is also an emphasis on individual expression and social interaction, so that children can discover their own personalities and learn to express them in relationships with others. Some parents also think that children should be praised indiscriminately, in order to bolster their self-esteem.

In the Chinese version, formal education makes people smarter. People who know calculus are smarter than people who cannot divide fractions. Formal education first teaches people how to divide fractions, and then algebra, and eventually calculus. At that point they are more intelligent than when they started out. Whatever strengths and weaknesses children begin with, the way for them to get smarter is to take advantage of formal education; and the way to do that is to work hard. When a child doesn't learn something, American parents may be thinking, "It's too bad he isn't smarter," while Chinese parents are more likely to think, "He'll just have to work harder." From this point of view, focusing on individual expression and social interaction is a waste of time that could more profitably be spent studying.

One weakness of the American version is that rote learning and memorization are not considered an important part of mastery. Unfortunately, not all learning is fun, and basic information has to be acquired in order to be able to make creative use of it. Another shortcoming is that children who don't show any special interests, talents, or abilities may be viewed as unlucky and left to languish rather than be pushed to achieve their "personal best." Setting too low standards out of concern for a child's self-esteem can be a counterproductive strategy.

One weakness of the Chinese version is that an excessive emphasis on hard work and practice may take the fun out of learning and stifle creativity. In addition, some parents may demand more of their children than they are capable of and thereby alienate them. An overemphasis on academic achievement may also lead to an underemphasis on social and emotional development.

So what is a reasonable strategy for fostering children's intellectual development? It is setting high but achievable intellectual standards, building on strengths, and working to improve areas of weakness. The way to do this is by rewarding good work and significant effort with praise. Effort is important, and it is better to try hard and not give up easily; but children also need to learn that actual achievement is the key goal.

In addition to communicating that school and studying and learning and thinking about things are important, the strategy involves providing intellectual challenges at the child's current level of competence. Tasks that are too easy are boring and set low standards; and those that are too hard can lead to failure and giving up. Those that are at the child's current level lead to a sense of accomplishment and merited self-esteem. For example, if a child who knows how to multiply two two-digit numbers can figure out how to multiply a three-digit number by a two-digit number—instead of being told how to do so—he or she will have the pleasurable sense of intellectual accomplishment and may view the next level as an attractive challenge.

In contrast to viewing intelligence as fixed and looking for biological explanations for group differences, the cultural perspective offers insights into why groups differ and educational strategies for raising more intelligent children.

CHAPTER 7

Dreams from My Daughter: Mixed Race Myths

Dreams from My Father gave a child's-eye view of Barack Obama's childhood. My parent's-eye view of raising a daughter under similar circumstances is aimed at illuminating questions faced by children of intermarriage. These include biculturalism and issues of racial and cultural identity.

Fishes and Obamas

In reading *Dreams from My Father*, I was struck by parallels between the family Barack Obama grew up in and the one my wife and I raised our daughter in. His book gave a child's-eye view of his upbringing; but this chapter is an attempt to offer a parent's view. Even after years in the public eye, President Obama is still seen as alien by many Americans, in part because of his unusual background. Perhaps the thoughts below will help to make his experience and that of children like him more comprehensible.

One way of looking at Barack Obama's youth is as the story of a boy, raised by a single mother and her parents, who by dint of hard work and natural gifts overcame great odds to become president of the United States. This is a true story.

Another way of looking at it is as the story of a person who, because his father was from Africa, looks black. Since he grew up in a white family, however, he had to overcome impediments to developing a racial identity for which American culture provides no easy answers. This is also a true story.

Yet another way of looking at it is as the story of a boy losing his Luo ties before he knew he had them, becoming an American in Hawaii, and then being uprooted and taken with his new family to Indonesia at the age of six, and then leaving them behind to return to Hawaii at the age of ten. Another true story.

Many people, including me, find these stories of triumph over adversity inspiring. Some others, when thinking of Barack Obama as our president, find them upsetting. Their anxieties stem in part from a fear of the unknown: an inability to imagine what someone with his background might actually be like. What can we expect from a man whose white Kansan mother married men from Kenya and Indonesia? Children make fun of names: shouldn't childhood ridicule—for his names, for not being simply black or white or Kenyan or Indonesian—have had a negative effect on his personality? What kind of effect could his mother's marriages and life in Indonesia have had on him?

True stories of overcoming adversity are not, however, the only possible stories. There is much that they omit. They seem to imply that Barack Obama's childhood was unique—which, as with all individuals, it was. But it is also true that others, including my daughter, share key aspects of his multicultural, multiracial upbringing, and that much is known about such children and their development. Obama's experience resembles theirs in many ways, and these commonalities can provide reassurance for those who are made uncomfortable by his unusual background. Marrying someone different isn't for everyone, but as with other life choices, it has advantages as well as disadvantages.

Stories of overcoming adversity omit this positive side—that of profiting from unusual opportunities for growth. *Dreams from My Father* was written from a son's perspective. My wife and I grew up at the same time as Barack Obama's parents, and we raised our daughter in a family with a number of parallels to his. While there are significant differences as well, the similarities between the two families are suggestive—especially in that my daughter and he share characteristics with other children who grew up in comparable circumstances.

During the spring of 1969, while I was a postdoctoral fellow in the SUNY Stony Brook psychology department, I met Dolores Newton, an African American anthropology instructor who had just returned from her second stint of fieldwork with the Krikati Indians in the interior of Brazil. I have to admit that it was Dolores's beauty that first caught my eye; but it was the fascination with someone so different from me that hinted at an interesting and potentially exciting life together. The better we got to know each other, the more unknown worlds we discovered. While black people in America have many experiences in all-white groups, few whites have had the corresponding opportunity. Getting to meet Dolores's family and friends gave me that chance and allowed me to see that, despite stereotypes to the contrary, blacks were actually more culturally varied than whites. In addition to people from the United States, there were immigrants from Latin America and the Caribbean, and even non-Westerners from Africa—while non-Western whites are hard to find.

Dolores and I read different books. We both had lots of records—mine were mainly Beethoven to Bartok, and the Beatles; hers were mainly Baroque, Folk, and Gospel. She played Marion Williams and the Stars of Faith for me:

Heart trouble, cancer, diabetes too,
If you need an operation God will give it to you.
He's a high-class physician. He guarantees his medicine too!

It was great music that I would never have come across without Dolores; its diction and enthusiasm were somehow missing from the halls of academe.

We were both social scientists, interested in understanding our fellow humans, but from the different perspectives of psychology and anthropology. (Ann Dunham became an anthropologist and Barack Obama, Sr. an economist.) People usually socialize with and are attracted to others like them and assume that their social reality is reality itself. Many social scientists find it interesting to question that assumption and see those who are different from them more as a source of new insights than of discomfort. One of the things that drew me to clinical psychology was the opportunity to come into contact with exotic phenomena such as delusions, hallucinations, and hypnosis. Dolores wanted to study living people who were as close as possible to our hunter-gatherer ancestors—and, by implication, as different as possible from us.

Even as social scientists, our contrasting perspectives were a source of continual surprise. We went to a party once, and in talking it over afterward it was as if we had been to two different parties—a Rashomon experience. I had noticed who was depressed or articulate or narrow-minded, while she had been paying attention to people's clothes as status markers.

One major difference between anthropologists and psychologists is that psychologists are very much of this culture, while anthropologists tend to be alienated from it. The anthropologist's fly-on-the-wall observer stance toward culture is sometimes misinterpreted as anti-Americanism by those who can't imagine what another culture might be like, or what the point might be of seeing the world through other people's eyes. It is as if the attempt to do so is disloyal or crazy. If looking at ourselves through the mirror of another culture reveals some warts, then that must mean that we think the other culture is more beautiful.

Ann Dunham married a Kenyan and an Indonesian, had children by them, and lived for years in Indonesia. It was as unlikely a path for a girl from Kansas, via the University of Hawaii, as was Dolores's from Bedford Stuyvesant via Harvard to Central Brazil. (A curious similarity is that their interests and PhD dissertations both dealt with material culture—things people make.)

One time, while we were dating, someone asked Dolores what the Krikati ate, and she mentioned bats, armadillos, and anteaters.

"What does anteater taste like?"

"It tastes a lot like monkey."

We were married in less than a year; and two and a half years later our daughter was born. While Dolores was pregnant, we gave a lot of thought to names. She thought that an American Indian name like Bearcat would go well with Fish, and for a while I was seriously considering Whirling Thunder as a boy's name. We considered foreign names—Lyudmila or

Oona. A friend of mine in graduate school had made up a satire on the MMPI personality test, and one of the items was, "Sometimes I say things that are too terrible to think." My mother said, "You aren't going to give her Krikati names, are you?"

A mother knows her son, and by that time she knew her daughter-in-law. We settled on Krekamey Ropkui, the names of two Krikati women Dolores had been close to and who had provided her with a lot of information. (Ropkui means Jaguar Woman.) I don't want to appear competitive, but when it comes to choosing names that do not conform to cultural expectations, there are lots of Barack Husseins in the world but only one Krekamey Ropkui.

When Krekamey was a few months old, I was carrying her around while grocery shopping. A little girl came up to me and asked her name. When I told her, she said, "Why didn't you call her Mary?"

Raising an Anthropologist's Child Abroad

From the time of our engagement, it was clear that Dolores and I would be spending significant time in Brazil. It took a few years to land visiting professorships; but finally in the spring of 1974 when Krekamey was twenty-two months old we moved to Campinas, a city of about one million in the state of São Paulo.

We rented an unfurnished apartment on the top floor of a high-rise in the heart of the downtown area. While the place had a few modern conveniences—closets—it lacked others that we had to provide. These included a refrigerator, a stove (running on gas canisters delivered to the door), and hot water (small electrical heaters had to be attached to the sinks and shower). There was no heat—Campinas has southern California weather, but when the winter temperature falls to 50 degrees, it is 50 degrees indoors too. So while life where we lived looked superficially similar to that in an American city—tall buildings, cars, people's clothes—once you got up close, everything was different, including the roosters crowing at dawn.

Krekamey had about two hundred words in her English vocabulary when we arrived in Brazil—and then everything changed to Portuguese. We enrolled her in a preschool, and within a few months she was transformed from an American child to a Brazilian one. I remember my frustration when she effortlessly used the future subjunctive correctly, while I was still struggling to speak rudimentary Portuguese. Meanwhile, her English sometimes deteriorated to "Portingles." One endearing sentence was "E quembody else vai come here?"—literally, "And whobody [by analogy to words like somebody or anybody] else is going to come here?" Because Krekamey's speech and nonverbal behavior were perfect, Brazilians often doubted that she was American—an illusion she furthered by refusing to speak English in public.

Krekamey's looks—or for that matter the appearance of our family—were quite normal in Brazil, and didn't provoke the curiosity we sometimes encountered in the States. On the other hand, when I was with Dolores and asked Brazilians a question, they would sometimes answer her—assuming from my accent and her looks that I was an American married to a Brazilian.

We spent July of 1975, when Krekamey turned three, with the Krikati. Their village is located about 350 miles southeast of Belem, the city at the mouth of the Amazon. The village consists of thatched-roof huts—some with two or more thatched walls, and some completely enclosed by four clay walls—arranged in a large circle with a diameter about the length of a football field. The interior of the circle is grass, except for a large, round ceremonial area in the center; and a number of well-trodden paths lead from one house to another or to the center. Chickens, some other domesticated animals, and a few scrawny hunting dogs wandered around or sought shelter from the sun. Dolores's census put the village population—from newborns to the oldest—at 215, with another 43 in a second, smaller scattering of houses in the forest. The Krikati could get to that settlement in a couple of hours, walking through light forest, but there were no clear trails or maps to show the way. That was it—the Krikati population, language, kinship system, oral history, customs, politics, art, religion, family life . . . you name it. Their complete social world consisted of 258 people, at least a fifth of whom were infants and young children.

The people, short and muscular by American standards, wore few clothes—both men and women were topless. Teeth filed to points, plucked eyebrows and eyelashes, and body paint all suggested a rather different aesthetic from that in New York or Campinas. There was a building called the *farmácia*—four walls and a roof, with a few benches but no medical supplies or other furnishings. As guests of honor we were invited to hang our hammocks there. It was a few nights before Krekamey woke up and realized that it wasn't birds that were flying around overhead.

"Mom, those are bats!"

"Yes, dear. Go back to sleep."

One morning, when we awoke, we saw that the benches were filled with people, looking silently at us. We were the most interesting thing around—a living television program.

Krikati kids have a great life. They roam around in bands and play for hours on end—no traffic, no crime, no pollution, no snow or ice. While I was serving as Dolores's research assistant cum family cook—making rice and beans in a pot over a single burner kerosene stove—Krekamey was off with the other kids. When we left the village, she was already speaking a few words of Krikati.

By the time we got back to the United States, at the end of the summer of 1976 when she was four years old, Krekamey's comfort with and intuitive understanding of cultural difference had become second nature. Black and white, United States and Brazil, American and Brazilian and Krikati—she had the idea that there are all kinds of people in the world, not only ones like those currently around her; and she shared with us the feeling that that was just fine. Although, despite our best efforts, she was losing her Portuguese and was becoming indistinguishable from other American kids, her cultural understanding remained, and she even used it to manipulate us. For example, when we were teaching her table manners she said, "I don't want to eat like Americans; I want to eat like Indians." What she meant was, "I don't want to use a knife and fork; I want to eat with my hands." That fall we went to visit Dolores's aunt in Boston, and Krekamey asked, "Do they speak English in Boston?"

Third Culture Kids

While my family's experience of bridging cultural worlds may not be typical, it is shared by others, including Barack Obama. Even without counting refugees and their families, who have special problems, the United States has huge numbers of immigrants, children of immigrants, intermarried couples, and children of intermarriage—all of whom live with cultural difference as a daily fact of life. In addition, a much smaller number of children grow up with significant experience outside of the dominant American culture, and there is even a term for them—Third Culture Kids (TCKs). These include "military brats" from bases around the world, as well as children of diplomats, missionaries, and those in multinational corporations. While their parents are engaged in work in a foreign setting (and become more or less cross-culturally adept in the process) TCKs go to school with the local kids, develop friendships with them, get to know their families, learn to speak the language fluently and accent-free, and generally could pass for locals (with the possible exception of not looking like them).

Among TCKs there is an even smaller subgroup who grow up in families whose main concern *is* with cultural variation itself—children of anthropologists and other social scientists. Krekamey and Barack Obama are in this subgroup.

Four Ways of Being Bicultural

Immigration, intermarriage, and the world of TCKs all present both the challenges and opportunities of culture contact. To oversimplify matters, there are four kinds of adaptations possible.

The best adaptation, exemplified by Krekamey, Barack Obama, and other TCKs, is a cultural "both/and." Kids who grow up in more than one culture can become adept at both. They might sometimes appear to others as (or even feel they are) cultural chameleons, but their perspectives from both cultures give them binocular vision—a unique asset in a complex world. They can serve as cultural interpreters or as bridges between cultures; and being able to experience the world in two ways gives them an intuitive understanding that there could be thousands of others. Living in another culture is stressful, and children of anthropologists have the advantage of a parent who can help them make sense of and profit from their experience. Krekamey can see the world through black and white eyes, and American and Brazilian eyes. It is something I envy in her. I came to other cultures as an adult, and had to work hard at developing a cross-cultural perspective. In comparison to her, I feel like a competent musician who has practiced diligently, but could never achieve the effortless performance of someone with natural talent. People similar to her—including, I believe, Obama—cannot help but understand and value other people's perspectives.

The second best adaptation is to identify exclusively with the dominant culture, and to reject or minimize the other one. Children of immigrants (e.g., my parents) who strive to be 100 percent American will do well because they are living in America—but they pay a severe price by rejecting not only the unattractive or awkward cultural features their parents brought with them, but also the cultural strengths. For example, when my father was a child my grandfather would speak to him in Yiddish, but insisted that he reply in English. This meant that speaking flawless American English was more highly prized in my father's family than bilingualism. Times were hard a century ago, and perhaps a goal of fluent bilingualism didn't seem worth the risk of cultural marginalization. But from my point of view, this should have been a no-brainer—two languages are better than one.

The third adaptation, which doesn't work well, is to reject the dominant culture in favor of the other one. Children of immigrants who reject American culture in favor of that of their parents' homeland are bound to be unhappy because, like it or not, they are in the United States, and American culture is omnipresent and inescapable. I am reminded of some of the wives of the male (they were all men in the 1970s) American executives who were living in Brazil. They socialized only with other Americans, didn't learn Portuguese or develop friendships with Brazilians, had trouble communicating with their maids, felt isolated despite their more affluent life in Brazil than in the States, and became depressed or took to drink or developed other problems. They suffered from their resistance to acculturation despite their evident money, power, and prestige.

The saddest adaptation, if it can be called that, is to reject both cultures. If some people like Krekamey (and, I believe, Obama) profit from the best of both worlds, others are overwhelmed by the worst. In America we have the stereotype of the tragic mulatto, rejected as an outsider by blacks and whites alike and acceding to a marginalized fate. Sadly, there are some such people, just as individuals can be found who are similar to other stereotypes; but their existence is by no means typical, nor does it prove the accuracy or inevitability of the stereotypes. If anything, Obama's presidency may encourage them to rethink their worldview.

Adults Who Were Children of Intermarriage

Despite their unique advantages, the very cosmopolitanism of adult TCKs sometimes leads them to feel rootless—unsure of their identity or of how to answer the question "What am I?" Surprisingly, in contrast to the fears of those who assume they are not American enough, their search for a rooted identity can make them more American than those who just do what comes naturally because that is all they know.

Krekamey's fair skin and ambiguous appearance left her the option of defining herself racially in various ways. Dolores and I raised her with the understanding that she could be whatever she wanted to be (and that others would let her be), but that she had to understand the racial situation in America in making her choice. If we had had more than one child, they might have labeled themselves in more than one way, and that would have been fine with us.

It was in college that Krekamey made up her mind that she was black (rather than mixed or bi-racial or even, conceivably though improbably, white—or refusing on principle to choose a label). As both her father and a social scientist, I have to admit that I was surprised by how much of a non-event this decision turned out to be. Neither her personality nor her interests changed. Like other TCKs, she had always had friends of varied backgrounds and hues and this continued to be the case—as it is to this day.

Ann Dunham was born two days after me, though in rather different circumstances. From what I have read, she was quite a woman—coming from the background she had and living the life that she did. I wonder if we passed each other in the corridor during a meeting of the American Anthropological Association. Barack Obama Sr. was born a year before Dolores. Perhaps Dolores and he walked by each other on the Harvard Campus during the fall of 1962. Dunham divorced twice, adding psychological and financial strain to the cultural richness she offered her children; and she and both of her husbands died young. Dolores and I have been married forty-two years; and Krekamey, who grew up on Long Island, says in comparing herself to some of her black friends that we raised her in a bubble. She did, however, major in Portuguese and Brazilian Studies and spend a year in Brazil before going on to become a pediatrician. In college she sometimes had the experience of knowing the meaning of Portuguese words without having studied them.

Intermarriages are common now, but we were pioneers back then. It is not surprising that Krekamey (and Barack Obama) might choose the rootedness of an African American identity over the global adventures open to a more ambiguously self-defined adult TCK. Krekamey married an African American architect, Christopher Craig, who was raised in Detroit, mainly by his grandparents, in more difficult circumstances than those of Michelle Obama's childhood. Like Michelle Obama, he is a man who has worked very hard to get where he is, and like her he is a monocultural American. In marrying Krekamey, he opened himself to a world larger than the one he grew up in.

CHAPTER 8

How the Myth of Race
Took Hold

This chapter reviews and extends earlier discussions of reasons that the human species has no biological races. It compares the spread of humans out of Africa over tens of thousands of years with the spread of the race concept out of Europe over a few hundred years. It also explains why the race concept is so durable despite scientific evidence to the contrary.

How Concepts Spread

In his 1976 book, *The Selfish Gene*, the biologist Richard Dawkins offered a creative idea. He proposed viewing Darwinian natural selection, which explains the origin, spread, and increasing complexity of life on our planet, as a more general principle that could be applied to any self-replicating system. Dawkins explicitly intended such systems to include abstract ideas as well as concrete objects. He coined the term *meme* to refer to culturally transmitted entities, such as "tunes, ideas, catch-phrases, clothes, fashions, ways of making pots or of building arches" (p.192), that spread and evolve through differential survival. As he put it:

> The gene, the DNA molecule, happens to be the replicating entity that prevails on our own planet. . . . I think that a new kind of replicator has recently emerged . . . still drifting clumsily about in its primeval soup, but . . . achieving evolutionary change at a rate that leaves the old gene panting far behind. The new soup is the soup of human culture. . . . (p. 192)
>
> Imitation, in the broad sense, is how memes can replicate. But just as not all genes that can replicate do so successfully, so some memes are more successful in the meme-pool than others. This is the analogue of natural selection . . . qualities that make for high survival value among memes . . . [are] longevity, fecundity, and copying-fidelity. (p. 194)

The idea is that a meme that makes lots of long-lived exact copies of itself will occasionally make an inaccurate copy. If that variant has a reproductive advantage then it will spread, regardless of its truth or beauty (though truth and beauty are among the repertoire of tricks memes use to spread themselves).

In her 1999 book, *The Meme Machine*, the psychologist Susan Blackmore developed the meme concept even more. Viewing humans as meme vehicles in much the same way that Dawkins views organisms as gene vehicles, Blackmore took "the memes' eye view" in exploring the meme concept and the evolution of increasingly complex meme forms and structures. The following are a few examples of her ideas.

Blackmore asks why it is that we always have something occupying our consciousness, including trivia, such as jingles from TV commercials that we would rather be free of. Her answer is that memes that grab our attention spread more effectively than those that do not and therefore crowd out the meme competition (as well as mental silence or emptiness). She also discusses a variety of reasons that some memes are better at grabbing our attention than others—examples of which are involvement with emotions or with biological needs such as hunger and sex.

Blackmore introduces the concept *memeplex*, or co-adapted meme complex, to describe memes that replicate better as a group than individually. Ideologies and religions are examples of notably fecund memeplexes. The *selfplex* is a key memeplex that evolved in the domain that psychologists and social scientists refer to as the self (including the self-concept, body image, and a wide range of related subject matter). Blackmore discusses gene-gene, gene-meme, and meme-meme co-evolution, and speculates in some detail on the role of memes in the evolution of the brain and the development of consciousness (a particular interest of hers).

Naturally, *The Meme Machine* was a provocative book and stimulated much debate, since the meme concept offers a controversial mechanism to explain the otherwise nebulous phenomena of cultural evolution and cultural diffusion. Criticisms of the concept include a demand for a precise, testable meme definition, and the complaint that definitions like Blackmore's "whatever is passed on when people imitate each other" are circular.

This complaint might have some traction when applied to ideas about meme-gene interactions in the evolution of the brain, since it would be advantageous to be able to specify the meme component of an interaction as clearly as the gene component. When it comes to the diffusion of cultural ideas and objects, however, I am less troubled by conceptual vagueness or circularity. In operant conditioning, for example, the definition of a reinforcing stimulus is circular—it is a stimulus that reinforces. Nevertheless, the concept of a reinforcer has been an extremely productive one, yielding all kinds of reproducible data about conditioning, extinction, generalization, schedules of reinforcement, and so forth. In a similar way, if the meme concept yields new data, empirical relationships, and theoretical insights about cultural phenomena (or anything else, including the brain and consciousness for that matter) then it should be regarded as a useful one. If all that the meme concept yields are words talking about words, then I'm afraid we will have to abandon it as not scientifically productive.

I will be using meme terminology when necessary, because it presents a unifying, conceptual framework for quite varied material. In addition, there may be explanatory value to viewing the spread of memes as a dynamic process propelled by Darwinian selection. This would be in contrast to merely observing that concepts spread (some more than others) and labeling the process *diffusion*. Despite this explanatory advantage, the validity of the points that I will be making and the overall thrust of my argument do not depend on the use of meme terminology (or jargon, depending on your point of view). For this reason, I will try to substitute non-technical words like *concept* whenever possible.

This book's main concept of interest is *race*. It is easy to see that race is a meme, and a rather important one at that. (Actually, it is a memeplex, though I will call it a meme for the sake of simplicity; and I will often use the shortened form when referring to other memeplexes, if a non-technical term is inadequate.) For example, the historian Niall Ferguson, in his book *The War of the World*, explicitly uses the term *race meme* in exploring its pivotal role in the bloody history of the twentieth century.

My aim here is both more limited than and different from Ferguson's. It is to contrast two elements so as to make clear that they are distinct phenomena. The first is the gradual migration of humans out of Africa and around the planet over tens of thousands of years, accompanied by the climatic adaptations and random genetic changes (genetic drift) that have led to variations in our visible characteristics—as well as non-visible characteristics. The second is the rapid migration of the race meme out of Europe over a few centuries, accompanied by cultural adaptations to economic, political, and social conditions.

Out of Africa

As was discussed previously, the broad outlines of the origin of modern humans in Africa, and their subsequent spread around the globe, have been known since Darwin. With new archaeological finds, and especially with new genetic techniques, the picture is becoming ever clearer and more detailed. Naturally, different methods within and between the disciplines of archaeology and genetics always produce somewhat different results. For example, each gene has a different history (e.g., mitochondrial DNA is passed down in the female line, and women can have only a limited number of children; the Y chromosome is passed down in the male line, and Genghis Khan fathered thousands, so that millions of men now carry his Y chromosome). In addition, groups that died out may leave archaeological remains but no genetic trace.

Here once again is the story in brief. Anatomically modern humans first appeared in East Africa about 200,000 years ago—a very short time, whether measured against the history of the planet, or of life on Earth, or of mammals, or even of primates. This brief timespan, compounded by a bottleneck about 70,000 years ago, when our species was nearly wiped out and our genetic variability was greatly diminished, is one of the reasons that we have no races in the biological sense. In addition, since we have been peopling Africa with our kind for all of human history, that continent contains the great bulk of the limited biological diversity found in our species.

About 60,000 to 100,000 years ago the first modern humans left Africa through the Middle East and went on to populate the Eurasian continent. Those who left Africa represented only a small proportion of the genetic diversity on the continent at the time—or even of people near the land bridge (now Egypt). Subsequently, about 12,000 to 15,000 years ago, during the last ice age when the level of the oceans was so low that humans could walk across the Bering Strait, a few people in northeastern Asia crossed into the New World, probably following game.

As this history makes clear, the simplest way to characterize human biological diversity is in terms not of races but of regions of variability. There is maximum biological variability in Africa (where we have been the longest), an intermediate amount in Eurasia (reflecting our intermediate length of stay there), and relatively little in the indigenous populations of the Americas (as a result of our recent arrival). If the human species did have biological races, they would all be in Africa. This is easy to see— remember the very short Pygmies, the very tall and lanky Masai, and the Bushmen of the Kalahari with large (steatopygous) buttocks and tufted (peppercorn) hair. It is only the Western cultural focus on non-white skin color that makes it possible to relegate these variations to lesser importance, and view all three groups as members of the same "black race."

Different physical features (e.g., skin color, nose and lip forms, and hair texture) and genes (e.g., for A-B-O blood types) do not vary together in "racial" syndromes. We can verify this by simply looking at the faces of people wherever substantial diversity exists—for example, as mentioned previously, on the New York City subway. In order to understand why this is the case, we need to briefly review two relevant concepts—breeding populations and clines.

Breeding Populations and Clines

As discussed in Chapter 1, a breeding population consists of members of a species that breed among themselves more frequently than they do with other members of the species. Over time, the breeding population comes to differ from other populations of the species in the frequencies of certain genes. In general, this distinctiveness arises through the mechanisms of mutation, natural selection, and random changes known as genetic drift.

We can compare the biological concept of breeding population with the concept of race. First of all, breeding populations are merely statistical subgroups of species, which may be defined in whatever way is useful for research purposes. For example, one might wish to examine populations characterized by 99 percent inbreeding over twenty generations (there are no such human populations) or one might investigate populations characterized by 51 percent inbreeding over two generations (there are millions of such human groups). Secondly, it is important to remember that all breeding populations belong to a given species. Humans from anywhere in the world, regardless of visible characteristics, are capable of producing fertile offspring with other humans from anywhere else. Finally, even when a group qualifies as a breeding population according to some statistical criterion, it can merge with other groups and cease being a breeding population in a single generation. Modern transportation has increased gene flow around the world, so that the number of breeding populations according to any given statistical criterion is rapidly declining.

It is easy to see that the biological concept of breeding population is different from the social concept of race to which we are accustomed. In particular, social judgments of race frequently include visible characteristics, such as skin color. Clearly, one cannot tell a person's breeding population from phenotypic information. Neither, however, can a person's breeding population be determined by knowledge of genotype. Suppose, for example, that 40 percent of the members of a purported race have the gene R, while 20 percent of other humans have the gene. The fact that a given individual does or does not carry the gene is of no help in deciding whether or not the person belongs to the breeding population in question.

Given the distinction between breeding population and the social classification of race, it is worthwhile pointing out that neither whites nor blacks constitute a breeding population. Whites are not a worldwide breeding population because whites in American breed with blacks in America more frequently than they do with whites in Australia or Russia. And blacks are not a worldwide breeding population because blacks in America breed with whites in America more frequently than they do with blacks in Ghana or Tanzania.

In contrast to blacks and whites, residents of an isolated small town are a good example of a breeding population because they do breed among themselves more frequently than with others. On a larger scale, all North Americans—including our entire diversity of visible characteristics—constitute a huge breeding population, since we do breed among ourselves more than with non–North Americans; and all Africans, including all of their diversity of visible characteristics, also constitute a giant breeding population for the same reason.

In examining the global distribution of different human physical features and genes, one discovers an interesting pattern. Not only do the different features vary independently, but each does so gradually and in different directions along lines known as *clines*. The reason for this pattern of gradual variation, as initially discussed in Chapter 1 and reviewed and extended here, is easy to understand. Suppose that several breeding populations are geographically situated along a line, where the members of A have some contact (including sexual contact) with those of B, B with C, and so forth. If the population of A begins with a high frequency of some gene, which is absent in the other populations, then it is likely that some of the offspring of their contacts with B will carry the gene. Since A and B are separate breeding populations, the frequency of the gene among the members of B will never reach its level among A. Some of the carriers in B will transmit it to the offspring of their matings with people of C, though the frequency of the gene among the members of C will never reach its level among B, and so forth. In this way, over many generations, the trait will spread out in declining frequencies the further one is from A.

The hodgepodge of clines, running every which way all over the globe does not suggest that humans consist of a small number of distinct "racial" entities that developed separately.

Rather, the data are more what one would expect from a species in which different groups migrated to all corners of the earth in differing numbers and at different times, splitting apart, becoming isolated, merging with new groups, and generally combining and recombining in myriad ways across time and space. The model of evolution that best explains human variation is not a branching tree, but rather a tangled lattice.

In summary, human physical variation is clinal, not racial. Because human variation around the planet is gradual, the more distant two populations are, the more different they appear. Even when populations look quite different from one another—for example, Norwegians, Nigerians, and Japanese—if you look at all the populations in between them the pattern of gradual variation becomes evident. (Many people in India, for example, have dark skins like Africans, black straight hair like East Asians, and European facial features.) In addition, if you travel in different directions you encounter different kinds of variations. This point was illustrated nicely several decades ago by the anthropologist Marvin Harris who had the bright idea of getting pictures of United Nations delegates and arranging them in an array corresponding to the geographic locations of their countries. The gradual shift in visible characteristics from northern Europe to tropical Africa and the different gradual shift in visible characteristics from Western Europe to East Asia were easy to see.

Out of Europe

In contrast to the spread of the human species from Africa, the race meme spread from Europe. Humans spread around the globe—throughout Africa, and from there to Eurasia, and then to the Americas and elsewhere, diversifying along the way—over many tens of thousands of years. The race meme spread from the European colonial powers to their colonies around the globe and eventually to most humans, diversifying along the way—over a few centuries.

As described in Chapter 1, the Age of Discovery in the fifteenth century put Europeans in contact with others who differed from them in many ways, including visible characteristics. At first these differences were explained by references to the Bible, furthering the spread of religious memes. The Enlightenment brought the beginnings of modern science and offered "scientific" explanations—a new set of memes—as a rational alternative. These early explanations, that included items of clothing and pejorative stereotypes as racial traits were, to modern eyes, embarrassingly ethnocentric, subjective, and arbitrary.

As discovery turned to conquest and slavery, the difference in visible characteristics of the subjugated populations from their masters provided a handy, ideological justification for inequality. Hence, political utility presented a powerful force for the spread of the nascent race meme.

England, France, Portugal, and Spain (not to mention other imperial powers) had differing governments and legal systems; colonized different places with different indigenous populations, ecologies, climates, and natural resources; and spoke different languages. Once the race meme entered the culture of a colonial power, linguistic barriers limited memetic interchange with other powers in a parallel to the way geographic barriers have always limited genetic interchange.

In my research, I investigated the way the concept of race and its organization into subcategories (what anthropologists call *folk taxonomies*) differs greatly from one culture to another. I did this by comparing eight partial folk taxonomies of race among former colonies of England (the United States and Jamaica), France (Haiti and Martinique), Portugal (Brazil and Cape Verde), and Spain (Puerto Rico and Ecuador). This comparison made it easy to see that people can change their race by getting on a plane and flying from one place to another. What changes are not their visible characteristics, nor for that matter their genes or ancestry, but rather the folk taxonomy according to which they are classified. As mentioned earlier, a 1970 study by the Brazilian Institute of Geography and Statistics asked a sample of Brazilians what color they were and received 134 different answers. These include terms in the black-white range for individuals viewed as between white and black (e.g., *morena, mulata*) as well as neither white nor black (e.g., *sarará, cabo verde*)—a concept difficult for Americans to comprehend.

Linguistic separation (accompanied by the geographical separation of colonies within a particular empire) enabled the proliferation of racial folk taxonomies to take place in response to local conditions. At the same time, a combination of linguistic separation, ethnocentrism, and a lack of cross-cultural experience prevented the development around the world of an awareness that the terms used to refer to race vary widely in meaning from one place to another—an ignorance that persists to this day. That is, words like "race" and "type" along with their cognates and related terminology have wildly different meanings (denotations, connotations, rules for social usage, and socio-cultural implications) in different places; but hardly anyone, except the few social scientists who study the issue (and immigrants who are bewildered by it), is aware of this significant reality.

Slavery was above all an economic system—enforced by a legal system that was backed up by the power of the state. For this reason, differing local issues, especially economic and political ones in the differing empires and their colonies, led to differing legal solutions; and their various codifications brought with them self-perpetuating legal systems of "racial" classification. These de jure taxonomies then played a significant role in the evolving folk taxonomies of everyday life.

Consider, for example, the common occurrence of masters who impregnated their female slaves. What was the status of the children? Were they slaves or free? Could they marry? Could they own or inherit property—including slaves? Answers—which varied widely—to questions such as these required the creation of legally defined categories according to which people could be classified.

There were also cultural and demographic differences. For example, half a millennium of Moorish control of the Iberian Peninsula led to a greater familiarity with a range of skin tones in Portugal and Spain than in England; and the much higher ratio of Africans to Europeans in Portuguese Brazil as compared to British North America led to differing issues in the regulation of slavery and differing classificatory solutions.

Since people of African descent are a minority in the United States, "the one drop rule" has the effect of excluding them from membership in the more prestigious white classification, and facilitates their exploitation. Since people of African descent are a majority in Brazil, a vague, diffuse system of classification, with lots of possibilities other than just black or white, protects the powerful minority (with more money and less melanin) by preventing the development of a unifying black racial identity. If the one drop rule were to exist in Brazil, it would be political dynamite—defining into existence a de facto oppressed black majority in many ways parallel to the de jure situation under Apartheid in South Africa. (I should mention in passing that class discrimination in Brazil is stronger than racial discrimination in the United States, though Brazilian racial discrimination is milder than ours—at least for people who would be classified in the United States as lighter skinned blacks. Brazilians like to portray the strong correlation between darker skin color and poverty as a byproduct of social class differences. To those at the bottom, the question of whether their misery stems from racial or class discrimination is not of great moment.)

Racism is a meme that is related to the race meme (and only incidentally to actual physical appearance). As a result, since the race meme differs in different cultures, we would expect racial discrimination and stereotypes to vary from one culture to another as well. This is in fact the case. For example, racism tends to increase as one descends the social class hierarchy in the United States, while the opposite is the case in Brazil, with a remarkable degree of "racial democracy" (as Brazilians refer to it) among the poor. Also, in American sexual stereotypes blondes are the most beautiful and sexy, while in the northeastern part of Brazil *morenas* are the most beautiful and *mulatas* are the sexiest.

We can also better understand why it is that racism persists decades after scientists have shown that there are no races in the human species. You don't need races. All you need is the race meme.

Race in Europe Today

The fascinating variety of race meme mutations that I found in former European colonies led me to be curious about the varieties of the meme in Europe. I reasoned as follows. The race meme, which incubated in Europe, proliferated and evolved over a few centuries because of its cultural utility. It was of only limited usefulness in making and enforcing social distinctions in Europe, where other observable memes like speech or dress were more striking. The race meme was most efficacious in the colonies, where slavery was widespread and where indigenous peoples and imported Africans looked physically different from Europeans. Consequently, a reasonable reconstruction would be to view a relatively limited range of race memes in Europe as having been acted on by natural selection in the various colonies, leading to a greater variety there.

As a result of this reasoning, my initial hypothesis was fairly simple. Because people in Western European countries today are less diverse than in their former colonies (e.g., along the dimensions mentioned above—governmental and legal systems; indigenous populations; ecologies, climates, and natural resources; and languages), I expected their racial folk taxonomies also to be less variegated. Specifically, I expected less variation in the race meme among England, France, Portugal, and Spain than I had found among their former colonial possessions—the United States, Jamaica, Haiti, Martinique, Brazil, Cape Verde, Puerto Rico, and Ecuador. In other words, since Europe began with less variety, and since there has been a more limited variety of environmental pressures in Europe over the last few centuries for meme mutations, there should be a lesser variety of post-Linnaeus forms of the race meme there.

I began interviewing Europeans from England, France, Spain, and Portugal with the idea in mind of producing four folk taxonomies of race that could be compared to the eight in my previous research. In addition, I also interviewed some people from Germany, with the aim of producing a fifth folk taxonomy. Given the centrality of a racist ideology to the country's Nazi past, I was curious about what form(s) the race meme might have taken several generations after the end of World War II.

I rapidly ran into complications stemming from the greater time depth of Western cultures in Europe as compared to Western cultures in the New World. For example, while Europe has nothing to compare with the hundreds of indigenous languages found in the Americas, within the majority population of each European country one finds a long-standing regional diversity of languages. Here are a couple of illustrative examples from each country (though many languages cross contemporary borders): France—Breton and Gascon; Germany—Bavarian and Frisian; Portugal—Galician and Mirandese; Spain—Basque and Catalan; United Kingdom—Gaelic and Welsh. Thus, the degree to which I could generalize the information I was getting—always a central issue with cultural data—was a real problem.

While working on this project, I began reading about memes, and the focus of my interest began to shift from a static comparison of folk taxonomies to the idea of a dynamic process of Darwinian selection as a description for the spread of the race meme.

Here is an example. One summer I took a Bavarian houseguest to a Long Island beach. As we sat on a blanket and watched the variety of New Yorkers parade before us, I would ask him what word Germans would use to describe people who look like this person or that. Time after time (e.g., for people who look South Asian ["Indian"] or Southwest Asian ["Iranian"] to me) he would say he had no idea, or that he rarely saw people who look like that in Munich. This was also his answer to questions like "What would you call someone with one parent of African ancestry and the other of East Asian ancestry—e.g., Tiger Woods. On the other hand, when I asked about the "white folks," his vocabulary suddenly became quite variegated—using words like *holländisch* (Dutch), *italienisch* (Italian), *englisch* (English), and similar ones.

In retrospect, the way that race memes mutate to make relevant distinctions within a given culture strikes me as a parallel to the way species evolve to fill ecological niches (e.g., mammal species appear to have proliferated following the extinction of the dinosaurs); and the protection against extinction offered by memetic diversity can also be seen as a parallel to the protection offered by genetic diversity. Thus, it may be useful to think of race memes as having mutated (and continuing to mutate) to fill social niches.

Here is an American example: the increase in black-white intermarriages, following enactment of the 1964 Civil Rights Act and the 1967 Supreme Court decision legalizing interracial marriage, has led to a shift in the folk classification of the offspring of such unions from *black* to a new *mixed* category. For example, nearly all Americans in my parents' generation would have considered Barak Obama black, while a substantial majority of my students have viewed him as mixed.

The *mixed* category has also continued to grow because of the upsurge of immigration (and intermarriages of immigrants and their children) from countries whose racial folk taxonomies are different from ours. As a result, "Other" has become the fastest growing Census category, especially among self-classified "Hispanics." (In the 2010 census 37 percent chose "some other race" and 6 percent chose "two or more races," for a total of 43 percent. In other words, nearly half of Hispanics don't fit into the census's categories of race.) While the government and census have been slow to participate in the evolution of the American race meme, the news media as leading meme replicators have already been doing so—for example, in the 2000 *Time* magazine special report on "Redefining Race in America."

As I interviewed Europeans, I began to get an impression that was more specific than my initial hypothesis of less varied racial folk taxonomies in the four countries of the Old World than in their eight former colonies. That is, it began to seem not only as if the Old World race memes were less varied, but also that they were more similar to the memes of their former colonies—in that ancestry was a more important principle than visible characteristics in England, with the opposite being the case in the countries of Latin Europe. For example, it was interesting to learn—from an interviewee from Toulouse, France—that an intermarried couple might have three children of different physical appearance who would be considered *blanc* (white), *métis* (half-caste, or mixed), and *noir* (black). Naturally, more detailed research would be needed to confirm this impression of a more specific relationship between the racial folk taxonomies of the former colonial powers and their former possessions—but it does make cultural sense.

Americans tend to see three areas—North America, Latin America, and Europe. While living in Brazil, I was surprised to discover that Brazilians have a different (and culturally more accurate) view consisting of only two parts—North America + Northern Europe, and Latin America (including Mexico and the Francophone regions of Canada) + Latin Europe. Thus, if some future researcher should pick up on these hints and undertake a comparative study of the race concept in Europe, it might be interesting to add Italy to the Latin countries investigated and the Netherlands to the Northern ones.

I might also mention that—despite the stereotype of Germans as a rational/logical people—Germany was the only country whose interviewees provided me with internally inconsistent information. This occurred regarding the use of terms such as *Rasse* (race—a taboo word), *ethnische Gruppe* (ethnic group), *Farbige(r)* (a colored person), and *Mischling* (a half-caste, or "mixed" person).

The reason for this difficulty is not hard to understand. Because of the country's Nazi past and people's desire to overcome it, race is a taboo subject. Thus, while Germans feel a special responsibility to be sensitive about the issue, their defensiveness has the effect of walling them off from the clarifications that could be provided by open discussion (e.g., of findings from biological and cultural anthropology, and evolutionary biology). In addition, to my American eyes, the German population seems to be overwhelmingly white. This means that, even in many large cities, Germans are not exposed to the range of physical variation that is common in the United States—or for that matter in England or France.

As a result of the expansion of the European Union, cultural interchange—including intermarriage—is likely to increase. It is also possible that national identities might be at least partially displaced by a European identity (assuming that the current economic crisis doesn't arouse old antagonisms). These trends point to increasing contact and competition among race memes from different cultures, a process that should be accelerated as English increasingly becomes a common second language. Whatever the meanings of *race* in Europe today, they are likely to change.

Race and the Self

Raising the question of national identity (another meme), leads to the broader issue of the selfplex and of the race meme within it. (Whenever possible without loss of clarity, I will use simpler terms *meme* or *concept* or *idea* instead of *memeplex*, and *self* instead of *selfplex*.) Susan Blackmore discussed the self-plex as follows:

> The selfplex permeates all our experience and all our think-ing so that we are unable to see it for what it is—a bunch of memes. . . . The memes inside a memeplex survive better as part of the group than they would on their own. Once they have got together they form a self-organizing, self-protect-ing structure that welcomes and protects other memes that are compatible with the group and repels memes that are not. In a purely informational sense a memeplex can be imagined as having a kind of boundary or filter that divides it from the outside world. We have already seen how reli-gions, cults, and ideologies work as memeplexes; we can now see how the selfplex works.

Researchers are often perplexed—I used to be myself—by the tenacity of the race concept in the face of contradictory ev-idence. In 1941, the anthropologist Ashley Montagu presented evidence that the human species has no races in the biological sense; and by the early 1960s this had become the dominant view within anthropology. Why has there been only a minimal spillover of this knowledge from science to everyday life?

Thinking in terms of memes as replicators helps us to un-derstand the phenomenon. For example, astrology memes are more widespread in our culture than astronomy memes, just as race memes are more widespread than cline memes. How-ever, astrology memes rarely play a significant role in the self (though some people's behavior is influenced by reading a daily astrology column). In contrast, the race meme is inti-mately tied to many other memes that make up the self.

The social psychologist Harry Triandis studied the self cross-culturally and found major differences, especially between individualistic and collectivistic cultures. Western cultures are individualistic to differing degrees and in differing ways, and they understand people as independent actors. Most other cultures, to differing degrees and in differing ways, view groups such as the extended family or tribe as the primary entities, and the self is defined by relationships with others in the group. Thus, the export of the race meme from the individualistic West to the rest of the world implies that natural selection will favor mutations that are better adapted to the more collectivist versions of the self that it encounters.

The following are some of the key aspects of the self that include the race meme; they hint at the pervasiveness of the race concept and help us to understand its refractiveness to competing scientific information (e.g., gradual variation around the planet of people's physical characteristics). Body image includes race, as do aesthetic and sexual reactions to one's own physical appearance and that of others. The race meme is part of ethnic identity. People believe or have heard that they are similar to members of their social group not merely because they have learned similar beliefs and behaviors, but because they share some biological essence transmitted through their blood or linked in some way to their visible characteristics. The race meme plays an important role in the autobiographical self. We all have implicit or explicit stories we tell ourselves about how we got to be who we are—made up of bits of memories, things we have heard about ourselves from parents and others, fantasy, and other sources—and the race meme is prominent in these stories. We have behavioral expectancies of ourselves that become at least partially self-fulfilling prophesies (e.g., regarding ability in academic areas, music, sports, or the visual arts) and the race meme is active in these expectancies.

Given these multiple entanglements of the race meme with the selfplex—not to mention with other replicators in the media and throughout societies around the world—we can see why the race meme is complex, multifarious, pervasive, and as a result tenacious, despite scientific evidence to the contrary.

In summary, humans migrated out of Africa and spread around the globe over many tens of thousands of years, with more distant populations generally appearing more different from one another than closer ones. The race concept migrated out of Europe a few hundred years ago and spread around the globe, with race memes from different languages generally making different distinctions. The race concept flourishes despite contradictory scientific evidence because of its pervasiveness and variety in cultures around the world and because of its linkages to multiple aspects of the self.

MORE . . .

Scientific Websites

The *Genographic Project of the National Geographic* (https://geno-
graphic.nationalgeographic.com/genographic/index.html) traces the
genetic roots of our species. It uses DNA evidence to reconstruct the
way *Homo sapiens* began in Africa and spread around the world. Evidence from genetics and archaeology agrees in painting that picture of
our common past, and in showing that the human species has no biological races.

The website for the American Anthropological Association's project, *Race: Are We So Different?* (http://www.understandingrace.org
/home.html) looks at the history of the race concept, the scientific
study of human variation, and the lived experience of race around the
world. The project concludes, based on multiple sources of evidence,
that the human species has no biological races. It also examines the
ways different cultures classify people into differing systems of racial
categories, and then use those classifications as a basis for treating individuals differently.

Scientific Statements on Race

A 1941 paper by the British American anthropologist Ashley Montagu was the first to propose that the human species has no biological
races. By the 1960s subsequent research made that the consensus view
among physical anthropologists and evolutionary biologists, and it has
remained so as ever more confirmatory evidence has accumulated over

the decades. At the end of the twentieth century, the persistence of un-scientific views about race among the general public led to the adoption of formal statements by scientific organizations. Here are two:

American Anthropological Association. (1999, adopted 1998). American Anthropological Association Statement on "Race." *American Anthropologist* 100(3), 712–713. (http://www.aaanet.org/stmts/racepp.htm)
American Association of Physical Anthropologists. (1996). AAPA Statement on Biological Aspects of Race. *American Journal of Physical Anthropology*, 101, 569-570. (http://physanth.org/association/position-statements/biological-aspects-of-race)

Museum Exhibits

All of Us Are Related, Each of Us Is Unique (http://allrelated.syr.edu/) is an exhibit that can be viewed in its entirety online. It was originally produced in French by the Department of Genetic Anthropology in Geneva but was translated into English and made available online by the cross-cultural psychologist Marshall Segall. As with the following exhibit, it deals with both biology and culture.

The American Anthropological Association's project, *Race: Are We So Different?*, includes a museum exhibit (to which I contributed to the panel *How Are People Like Avocados?*). The exhibit, which has traveled to major science museums around the country, can be viewed at http://www.understandingrace.org/about/virtour.html.

Other Books on Race by the Author

Fish, J. M. (Ed.) (2002). *Race and Intelligence: Separating Science from Myth*. Mahwah, NJ: Lawrence Erlbaum Associates.
Fish, J. M. (2011). *The Concept of Race and Psychotherapy*. New York: Springer Science + Business Media.

ACKNOWLEDGMENTS

Over the years, many people have helped me in my work to understand race better and to communicate that understanding to others. These include individuals from various countries whom I have interviewed to learn about their ways of thinking about race, graduate research assistants who helped in a variety of ways, and friends, colleagues, and editors who have read over drafts of my earlier work, especially the two books listed above, and who offered me the benefit of their critiques.

I want to make special mention of a few individuals who contributed specifically to this book. Dolores Newton, my wife and anthropology consultant, who opened up the worlds of race and Brazil to me, gave me helpful comments on the manuscript's content. Robert Ghiradella, my former English professor, friend of fifty years, poet, and compleat artist, read over the manuscript and—as always—gave me helpful writing suggestions. John Adamus, leader of the Northern New Jersey Writers Group, has been instrumental in helping me make the transition from academic writing to writing for a broader audience; and members of the group have offered useful comments. Joëlle Delbourgo, my literary agent, has been a helpful guide to entering the culture of publishing and to bringing this work to fruition.

An earlier version of Chapter 8 appeared in my book *The Concept of Race and Psychotherapy* (listed above, pages 29–40), and earlier versions of many of the additional pieces appeared in *Psychology Today* in hard copy and/or online, or were built on passages from Chapter 1 of my book *Race and Intelligence*.

ABOUT THE AUTHOR

Jefferson M. Fish (PhD, Columbia) is Professor Emeritus of Psychology at St. John's University, New York City, where he has served as department chair and also as director of the PhD Program in clinical psychology. Dr. Fish is the author or editor of eleven previous books, including *Race and Intelligence: Separating Science from Myth* and *The Concept of Race and Psychotherapy*. He is also the author of more than one hundred journal articles, book chapters, and other works. Dr. Fish has served on the editorial boards of eight journals in the United States, Brazil, and India, and in a variety of roles for the International Council of Psychologists, the New York Academy of Sciences, and other academic and professional organizations. His website is jeffersonfish.com, and his *Psychology Today* blog is *Looking in the Cultural Mirror*.

Made in the USA
Las Vegas, NV
22 May 2021